THE
FOUR
AGES
OF
MUSIC

THE FOUR AGES OF MUSIC

by WALTER WIORA

Translated by
M. D. HERTER NORTON

W · W · NORTON & COMPANY · INC · New York

CONTENTS

ILLUSTRATIONS
following page 128

COMPARISON OF THE FOUR AGES IN PICTURES

ILLUSTRATIONS

SOURCES OF THE ILLUSTRATIONS

This translation owes much to the patience and approval of the author of *Die vier Weltalter der Musik;* to the knowledge as well as the editorial skills of Nathan Broder; to penetrating discussion of substance, argument, and language with Daniel Crena de Iongh.

M.D.H.N.

INTRODUCTION

Music is not a prerogative of the Western world and music history is the history of not only Western music. Basic forms of monophony and polyphony were cultivated even in the Stone Age; notable types of rhythm, of tonal systems, of musical philosophy evolved in pre-classical Antiquity, and in the later Orient; and all continents have been taking part in the musical life of today's industrial civilization and its technical evolution. This process in its entirety should be the theme of musicological research today; the thousand years of music in the Western world form only a particularly important part of the whole.

In widening its horizon to take in this whole, music history has been pursuing the new ideas and achievements manifest in the universal approach to world history [1] and to art history.[2] It must renew the 18th-century tendencies toward a universal view that looks beyond Europe, breaking through the confines of individualistic and nationalistic ideologies.[3] Not until we see Western music in the setting of universal history will we be able to understand its special position or to reach a knowledge of the present that will enable us to deal adequately with the wide trends in which we are involved.

[1] Cf. Leften Stravrianos, ed., *The Global History Series*, 1964 ff.; *Historia mundi*, 1952 ff.; *Propyläen Weltgeschichte*, 1960 ff., and others.
[2] Malraux and Salles's *Univers de l'art*, 1960 ff.; Heinrich Lützeler's *Weltgeschichte der Kunst*, 1959, or the *Pelican History of Art*, 1956.
[3] Cf. the author's "Musikwissenschaft und Universalgeschichte," *Acta Musicologica*, XXIII (1961).

How can processes like the spread over the whole earth of Western melody and harmony, or the leap of Asiatic and African peoples into global industrial civilization be understood if one sees them only in close perspective? What is happening today and how it is happening is of another sort than those transformations that took place within the Western world around 1300 or 1600, which are often referred to as analogous. The historical views heretofore presented in writings about music correspond neither to its present stage of development nor to the state of our historical awareness. A more universal picture has become necessary.

The present volume is not a handbook but, inasmuch as it calls attention to the total process and its constructive elements, a basic outline. A panorama with thousands of names, like an encyclopedia or a music history in many volumes, it cannot be in any case because of its brevity. But it means to throw light upon the whole as a whole and to help work out from the multiplicity of its factors the structure of that whole, much as in the analyzing of a symphony through a confusion of impressions one comes to recognize the structure of the composition.

Like a symphony, the course of music history takes shape in four "movements." The word Age is here used to distinguish these major periods from periods of smaller dimension, such as the Baroque or the Hellenistic. Our foursome of Ages does not follow traditional lines honored since Hesiod and the Bible, but derives from the facts. Alfred Weber has laid out the periods of world history in a similar manner, yet in music Western culture from the early Middle Ages to the early 20th century assumes a distinctive position, standing out more sharply from the other high cultures in this field than in art and literature. These thousand years of Western music form an Age by themselves.

In other ways too the special world of music is distinct in its nature and its growth from other realms of art and of life. Not until late was music set down in written characters and only later still did it achieve existence in fully notated works of art. The rational exploration of this special world that to many still seems irrational, was a central feature in its evolution, particularly in the Western Middle Ages. As *ars* or *scientia musica* it developed much as did the other sciences in antique and medieval times, in a manner different from the plastic and pictorial arts. With the 18th century, on the other hand, it served as a field especially for the counter-movements against the aridity of rationalist Enlightenment. In no sense has it been the eternal late-comer, even though certain cultural currents, like Humanism and Romanticism, prospered later in music than in literature. And how fruitfully and characteristically these currents found expression in music, so that there can be no question of a mere following after; how original and creative, indeed, Viennese Classics like Mozart and Beethoven seem in comparison with the Classicism of a Canova or a Thorwaldsen!

It goes counter to our historic conscience and our knowledge of universal history to exclude from music history the music of primitive peoples and of the Orient simply because that music seems relatively lacking in historical evolution and historical data. To leave it entirely to ethnomusicology, and to regard this as in essence a non-historical discipline, is impermissible, if only in view of the changes going on today in which primitive peoples and the high cultures of the Orient are mingling like streams in the ocean of general industrial culture. The distinction between historical and non-historical culture is far too rough as regards the various degrees of historical activity. Events of universal importance were followed in only a few places by further dynamic developments, in most merely by conformity to preserved tradition. Thus the creative growth that took place during prehistoric and early times was carried further by the high cultures, while primitive peoples took over, mixed, and altered prehistoric and early forms. Similarly, while ancient Greek music theory spread through the Orient, it was nowhere so systematically developed as in the *ars musica* of the West.

If one combines the study of surviving tradition with that of origins and takes into account regional as well as temporal divisions, one may picture the range of music history in its entirety as consisting of the following four periods:

I. Prehistoric and early times with their survivals among primitive peoples and in the archaic folk music of high cultures.

II. The music of the high cultures of Antiquity, from the Sumerian and Egyptian to the late Roman, as well as its manifold continuations and further developments in the high cultures of the Orient.

III. The musical art of the West since the early Middle Ages, which is distinct from that of the other high cultures through its polyphony, harmony, large forms (like the symphony), and other characteristics.

IV. Music in the technical and industrial Age, spanning all countries of the world, uniting the heritage of all previous cultures in a kind of universal museum and carrying on its international concert life, as well as further developments in technique, research, composition, and so forth, before a world public.

The history of an art is no mere structureless stringing together of changes in taste and ideas resulting in a potpourri of styles. Even fashions do not change in such primitive succession. Far-reaching connections, rather, extend through time and space. In the first place there are traditions, which wander through vast areas over a long time—from the most ancient cultic melody, for example, to the liturgical singing of today's church. Further, there are the constants of country, nationality, and other social communities. But especially there are lines of development, as, for example, the evolution of notation in the Middle Ages or of harmony in modern times. Much as such processes are modified by the variety of human groupings and by regressive currents, a main direction persists in them. For example, a trend appears in the making of musical instruments that begins with the alterations worked on objects found in Nature, like bones and horns, this having been preceded by the generation of rhythmic sounds by striking the body, stamping, hand-clapping. Thereafter more and more, as Arnold Gehlen phrases it for the history of culture in general, "organic material was replaced by artificial materials, organic force by inorganic forces." From singing bones and wooden drums the way led over clay drums to instruments of metal, later, for example, to keyboard instruments—e.g. the organ with its mechanical wind supply—and in the Technical Age to the electronic generation of tone (cf. illus. 3a-e). This way is to be represented not as a straight line, but as following many and various tracks.

The written notation of tones was itself prepared through body movements, signs made by hand and arm, "chironomy." It developed from vague signals that supported and needed to be supplemented by oral tradition, into independent notes freed of memory and tradition. At first it fixed only the central components—succession of tones, rhythm—later tempo also, dynamics, manner of performance. Simultaneously with these last, the shaping of all these elements was taken over more and more by the composer. His share in music as it was played and heard increased, while that of the performing musician shrank until he became purely an interpreter, obligated to "serve the work." Only in the musical art of the West did the score achieve supremacy. And now in our century the record and other new means of holding music fast are taking over. These are maturing new forms through which the music of this technical and industrial Age is distinguished from that of all preceding cultures.

The musical examples and the plates in the Appendix are intended to illustrate as clearly as possible within so brief a volume the connections and the differences mentioned above, and especially the contrast between the four Ages. The Bibliography has been limited to more recent writings not only because of space but also to emphasize the present state of our knowledge and the trend in musicological research. Most of the works listed have appeared within the last years, a few in the fourth and a very few in the third decade of our century. The English edition has been altered in a few places from the German and the Bibliography increased by a few recent titles. I am grateful to M. D. Herter Norton for the excellent translation.

 I

THE FIRST AGE

PREHISTORIC AND EARLY PERIOD

 1

PREHISTORY AND THE
QUESTION OF ORIGINS

Prehistory is the overture to world history. It precedes the periods to come not as the tuning-up of instruments precedes the concert, but as the first movement of a symphony precedes the following movements. That is why it is indispensable for an understanding of the whole course of history: as Friedrich Behn has said, "one cannot understand a drama without the first act or a symphony without its first movement."

This holds for prehistory as an independent discipline and for the prehistory of plastic and pictorial art, both of which have undergone a particularly fruitful growth since the discovery of Stone-Age cave paintings and other remains; but does it also hold for the prehistory of music? Are not the sources here too scant, and are not the theories hitherto thought up about the origins of music mere speculations without scientific value?

The prehistory of music can indeed not draw at an overflowing fountain, yet its situation is not hopeless. Many insights may be gained that reach out far beyond the state of our knowledge heretofore, if, in the first place, we ask more competent questions than before, secondly, call upon all available sources, including traditions surviving in the most primitive societies of today, and, thirdly, employ better methods in exploiting these sources.

1. The purpose of such investigation is to seek, not *the* origin of music as a unique event, but rather the multifarious origins and beginnings of rhythm, tonality, polyphony, of instruments, of the musical sense, and so forth. Its field is the whole period which preceded the rise of the first high civilizations in Mesopotamia, on the Nile, and on the Indus some 3,000 years before Christ, and which in all other parts of the earth endured for a shorter or longer time. In Europe, particularly in the areas remote from the Mediterranean, this early period extends over the Neolithic as well as the Megalithic, the Bronze, and the Iron Ages, into the Christian era. Among primitive peoples and in some archaic styles of folk music, remnants of it still survive today.

Music is a game with tones; through definite or halfway definite pitches and tone relations it is distinguished from pre-musical and partly musical sound, such as recitative and rhythmic noises produced with rattles, bullroarers, and other resonant objects. But it is from sounds of this sort that it developed and among primitive peoples it was and still is interspersed with and surrounded by them. Rootbed and environment for primordial music, furthermore, are provided by the sounds of nature, such as the tones and rhythms in the answering calls of birds and animals, recently transcribed by zoologists in their comparative study of animal voices.

Speculations about the origins of music have a lasting value, not indeed as knowledge, but as stimuli to investigation. Cries and expressions of feeling, speech, shouting, and calling certainly were factors that must have played a part, as well as the instincts of sex and self-preservation, joy in play and other psycho-physical impulses. For the development of regular rhythm, uniform body-movement executed in common in dance and cult was essential, rhythmic work as such coming up much later than music.

2. Among our sources, objects discovered in excavations are indeed far sparser than those residues that have survived in the life and use of today's primitive peoples, but they can be more accurately dated. Besides instruments there are rock paintings of magicians, mask-dancers, and rites. Primitive music was interwoven with supramusical activity and must therefore be investi-

gated in connection with research into cult, dance, and shamanism.

The importance of surviving traditions is obvious, especially since Carl Stumpf's foundation-laying book, *Die Anfänge der Musik* (*The Beginnings of Music*, 1911). Surely much has been preserved among today's primitive peoples that reaches back into the most ancient periods of human culture; comparative methods make it possible to distinguish it from all those accretions that further development, the influences of high cultures and sometimes of reprimitivization later brought with them.

A third important source lies in myths in which archaic motifs are preserved, myths about the origins of music or the fable of the "singing bone." [1] There are in addition other types of sources, particularly reports written in the high cultures of Antiquity about then primitive peoples, as well as conclusions drawn from early music about still earlier music. No one of these sources is sufficient by itself; taking them together and in combination we may be able to arrive at facts not immediately given.

3. This is difficult, but it is also one of the attractions of musicological research into prehistoric times. The most ancient of mankind's music is not accessible and palpable—as are, for example, cave paintings of the Stone Age or compositions that since the Middle Ages have been written down—but it must be sought out and revealed. This requires strict methods of comparative research like those comparative philology has developed in drawing its conclusions about older languages and cultures from languages still extant. Most fruitful are comparisons between backward areas that are widely separated and maintain no traffic or cultural exchange but may have common roots. Old Siberian and South African hunting tribes, for example, independently of each other have preserved cultural elements of Stone-Age hunting peoples.

How imperative it is to exercise care in historical interpretation of surviving traditions is shown from the criticism directed against the *Kulturkreislehre* of Fritz Graebner, Wilhelm Schmidt, Oswald Menghin, and others, who prematurely set up a comprehensive

---

[1] According to this widespread motif one of a murdered man's bones was fashioned into a pipe which when played upon gave forth a song that told of the murder and the murderer.

system of cultures and their historical connections on the grounds of similarities they presented. Similarly, the assumption that the further away from their cradle cultural elements are found, the older they must be, is untenable. His application of this criterion and of the *Kulturkreislehre* had a detrimental influence on the works of Curt Sachs, that outstanding pioneer in the universal history of music. But while doubts about methods may be justified, a sterile rejection of all historical ethnology is certainly not, as is evident from newer contributions to the field. [2] Moreover, the archeological and ethnological sides of prehistory are drawing much closer together than before. Research into prehistoric music depends on this alliance, and the task that lies ahead will be to follow it through methodically all along the line.

Music did not spring all at once into full being, but little by little. It had to win through against other basic forms of sound production that were partly musical, like rhythmic noise or speech without melody.

Thus one way led from pre-musical noise-makers through intermediate forms—such as flutes in which two or three holes were bored without aiming at exact intervals and "tuning" of the instrument—to musical instruments on which melodies could be played. Another way led from a sliding or slurring movement of the voice to partly musical singing in which some intervals are already fixed, and later on to full melody in which the voice adheres entirely to definite steps, e.g. as in a pentatonic scale.

It would be arbitrary to declare any one of these stages in its development to be the beginning of music, or simply to attribute the origin of music to the Greeks because it is from them that the name and concept of *technē mousikē* first stems. If we call music in the broadest sense every playing with fixed tone values, this was already well developed in the Upper Stone Age—at least in the last phases of that age, in a time over 30,000 years ago. Its primal forms are probably earlier still, for it belonged as an element in those cultic dances that we have good reason to assume

[2] E.g. Kunz Dittmer's *Allgemeine Völkerkunde* (*General Ethnology*, 1954).

preceded the plastic and pictorial arts. And these may already have evolved some 60,000 years before Christ, in the middle Aurignacian period. Even at that time flutes already existed.

MUSIC IN THE
HUNTING CIVILIZATIONS
OF THE UPPER STONE AGE

The history of high culture begins around 3,000 B.C., that of village culture two or three thousand years earlier. The time-span from this beginning of regular cultivation of the soil and permanent settlement of communities to the present technical age thus does not yet cover 10,000 years. The period from the beginning of settlement back to the beginnings of art, on the other hand, is some six times as long. In these five times ten thousand years man lived as a wandering food-gatherer and hunter. He hunted game in the wilderness, but was himself not "wild"; for he had already formed cults, evolved customs, made himself objects, and the substance of all these activities may, without stretching the word too far, be described as culture.

From the last stage of the Upper Stone Age, which in Europe lasted from about 25,000 to 10,000 B.C., we have sculptures and rock drawings of a high level of workmanship. They show how untenable is the notion that for those early times we need reckon only with quite simply primitive achievements. Despite many differences, the art of the Franco-Cantabrian civilization has features in common with the partly later cave paintings of Spain and North Africa. The mode of life in these communities was also broadly similar; they were no longer hunters and food-gatherers of a low order, bringing down game at close quarters with stones, traps, and simple spears, but hunters of the steppe of a higher grade, who attacked animals like bear, bison, and reindeer with arrows and spears flung from a distance, and sought in their cult to exert control over their relation to such big game. Spiritual center of the group was the sorcerer-priest. By his artistic power and achievement he often stood out well above the average, as later the charismatic individual was to do among the members of his group. The prototype, as yet not specifically differentiated, of singer, musician, and artist, he led the group in performing their rites or himself carried these out; it must have been such sorcerer-priests who made the paintings and the sculptures. Shamans and medicine-men among races that have preserved cultural elements of these prehistoric hunters of the steppes still represent this type, which can be in part discerned and in part deduced from Stone-Age arts. They dance in animal masks, draw pictures with magic significance on rock walls or shamans' drums, shoot at these pictures in ritual manner with bow and arrow, and conduct cult ceremonies, such as initiation.

The mimetic dances in animal masks represented in certain rock pictures evidently had ritual significance; the round-dance, of which traces have been preserved in impressions of the heels of young people in the clay floor of the Tuc d'Audoubert cave near Montesquieu-Avantès (Ariège), is interpreted as an initiation ceremony performed before a pair of sculptured bison. That such dances were older than their representation in pictures is clear from one fundamental consideration. Man is primarily a creature of action, and the movements of his own body would precede their objectified representation in wood and stone. That such dances and rites were widespread among the most primitive peoples also bears this out. Accordingly, too, prehistorians like Henri Breuil and art historians like Hans Sedlmayr agree in assuming that the Stone-Age hunters first acted out the animal and their real or mythical relation to it and only later objectified and held these fast in their rock art. Mimetic preceded plastic representation. The acting out of the fight with the animal has been called the oldest drama and the oldest art, and one assumes also that myth in its original form was dramatic and that myth as story appeared only later.

Now dance and pantomime are not carried out in silence by primitive peoples; body movements belong, together with vocal activity and the rhythmic resonance of hand-clapping and foot-stamping, to such group performances. The early magician too, as is to be seen from the way he is represented in rock paintings, evidently made every effort to enhance his magic power in manifold ways; like the shamans and medicine-men in surviving primitive societies, he would surely not have failed to make use of the numinous penetrating quality of the voice but would have exploited it no less than the visible spectacle. In addition to noise-makers, furthermore, the Upper Stone Age had developed instruments with fixed tones, especially pipes and musical bows. In a picture in the Trois Frères cave (a neighboring cave to the Tuc d'Audoubert) a magician is playing on the type of bow that has survived among many African peoples, including Bushmen, as the musical bow (cf. illus. 2a). A later rock painting from Southwest Africa shows a procession of four women with musical bows (illus. 8a). Taking all these evidences and criteria into consideration it is certain that these rites had musical elements. Herbert Kühn and other prehistorians even assume that in those days as in later cultic life music "played a large role."

It resounded not only across free open spaces—namely the steppes—but also in echoing enclosures—namely caves, those natural forms of the church and crypt to come. It was therefore a prehistoric cult music and should not be imagined as a fresh and lively music of the hunt with halloo and the sounding of horns. It belonged primarily not to the real chase, but to those rites in which the community celebrated its pretotemic relationship with bison or bear and thus established its own permanent attitude towards the world. Thus was carried out the continual inner conflict between the urge to self-preservation and the sense of guilt, for one killed with a bad conscience, chiefly because man at this time distinguished the manlike animate creatures he was killing less sharply from himself than he did later. Thus in the bear-ceremonial still preserved among Old Siberian tribes the slain bear is greeted with singing and begged for forgiveness.

In the Lower Stone Age man had not yet tamed animals as in the later cattle-raising times, but he sought to bind them to himself. Voice and sound played their part in winning inner power over an animal opponent. The same picture in the Trois Frères cave represents not a real hunt but a mythical scene of enticement and capture. This is apparent at once from the fact that one of the animals is half deer, half bison, and the other, a reindeer, has been given the webbed feet of some aquatic bird. Races among which Stone-Age hunting customs have survived, like Pygmies, Eskimo, and Indians, impersonate wolf, buffalo, reindeer in round-dances with singing: they imitate the movements and the voices of these and other animals. Miming and reality were not kept clearly apart: with a mask one psychically "changed" oneself into the creature one was playing.

Taking into account all these contexts with which music was interwoven as a factor, one would hardly interpret the pipes and flutes in evidence since the Aurignacian period exclusively as instruments for communicating with hunting companions or for enticing game. In that prehistoric world of belief a bone, a piece of an animal, must generally have been regarded not merely as a useful signalling implement but rather as a "singing bone," as in the later fable. Probably two ideas merged here: the sound the magician magically brought forth from the bone was the voice of the creature the bone conjured up, together with everything it stood for, and secondly with this sound one achieved power over creatures of this kind. Often animals were pictured on such bones, or symbols drawn. The fact that simple pipes were not discarded after the flute with holes became widespread also speaks, as Hermann Moeck has noted, for their cultic significance. A further argument against their general use as merely utilitarian signal pipes lies in these simple pipes having sometimes been made of human bones.

What applies to bones may also be true of horns and other parts of animals. Perhaps animal horns like the one the sculptured "Venus" of Laussel (near Marquay in the Dordogne) holds in her hand were blown even in those days. Various implements probably served for producing noises or tones beside other uses, just as Australians beat boomerangs together in their nocturnal dances and knock with sticks upon their spear-slings. Perhaps too, prehistoric spear-slings or throwers were used in this sense; not a few of the examples found are so exquisitely ornamented and so fragile that one thinks of them as ritual implements rather than weapons. The so-called "commando-staves" also, in view of their artistic form and finish seem destined rather for ritual than for use. Kirchner considers them to be sticks for pre-shamanistic drums and other prehistorians assume the same of some of these implements. That wooden and skin drums already existed at that time, before the Neolithic clay drum, is probable in view of their diffusion among very primitive races as well as for intrinsic reasons.

It is significant that the bow, the main weapon of those long-range hunters, was used for producing tones. It first appears in the rock painting already referred to in the Trois Frères cave (illus. 2a) played upon by a magician. This is no flute, but both a shooting and a music-making bow, which is fastened to the mask and struck with the right arm. The connection between shooting bows and music in later myths has often been pointed out. Thus Apollo is god at once of music and of archers. Plutarch reports that at their feasts the Scythians played upon their huntsman's bows as upon musical instruments. Very like the primitive magician is the Old Siberian shaman who threatened spirits and shot at them with his bow used as a cultic tool. Elsewhere too among primitives the bow has remained a primitive musical instrument, while higher cultures have developed it into other stringed instruments.

A promising way of finding out about the music of these Eurafrican steppe hunters of the Stone Age lies in comparing the traditions of similar hunting races in northern Eurasia and South Africa today. On the one hand, customs and cultural elements of the Stone-Age hunters, especially the bear ceremonial, have been preserved in Siberia among the Samoyeds, Ostyaks, Voguls, and so forth. Closely related to Old Siberian races are the Lapps, who probably migrated from the East into Finno-Scandinavia soon after the end of the Ice Age; later they did take to reindeer breeding, but they retained older substrata of the Stone Age and among these certain types of narrative song, the *Joikku*, obviously belong, particularly those concerning animals and the magic relationship with them.[1] On the other hand, corresponding traditions are to be noted in South Africa, and that among ancient Khoisanid, or click-language, populations, especially the Bushmen and Pygmies; these at one time roamed over much broader parts of Africa, but were later driven back into primeval forest and desert steppe by the growth of the Negro peoples after the close of the Ice Age. The Bushmen, descended from the stronger and larger Proto-Bushmen, have carried on the art of rock painting into our day. According to Yvette Grimaud and Gilbert Rouget, Bushmen and African Pygmies have certain common traits in their music and dance that can be explained not as taken over by the one from the other, but only as springing from a common root.

Much less can we reckon with influences from these Bushmen and Pygmies living so far to the south upon the Siberians and Lapps way up north, or vice versa. So much the more significant is the similarity in certain basic features of their music (cf. music exx. 4 and 5). These form a style that, being a peculiar complex of various characteristics, is by no means universally widespread, and surely did not arise polygenetically in different places on the earth. Such common features are: bi- to pentatonicism (i.e. melody having only 2, 3, 4 or 5 steps to the octave, with predominance of the main consonances: fifth, fourth, and octave); frequent oscillation of the voice to the fifth, sixth, and other intervals (e.g. c-g-c-g . . .); fairly wide vocal range and leaps of large intervals, mobility of the voice and rapid traversing of the octave; "flung" tones (*Schleudertöne*); frequent changes of vocal register, yodeling and similar devices; singing on vocalises; expansion and contraction of intervals in the repetition of motifs.

Such a complex of features with its characteristic breadth and mobility well befits the general bearing of these Stone-Age steppe

[1] The collections of Armas Launis, Karl Tirén, and others offer a rich picture of these songs.

hunters. That it should first have developed only later among Siberians and Bushmen is gainsaid both for the reasons just mentioned and by the fact that these people, while they preserved much, were never outstandingly creative. If the style actually does go back to those Late Paleolithic hunting cultures in which the important art of rock painting was invented, it gives us a vantage point from which to clear up somewhat the musical development that preceded it.

We have proof that the flute was extant much earlier, in the Aurignacian period, and not just the pipe of reindeer bone, which may already have been present in Protolithic times, but the flute with fingerholes as well, which some scholars believe must stem from a high culture. Consequently music of fixed pitches, with clearly differentiated tones, must reach back at least into the Aurignacian. In what order these sounding points were arranged and grouped can only be inferred from comparison with surviving traditions, although ornamentation and drawings from the various phases of the Paleolithic show how the visual concepts of point and rhythm, sequence and grouping were dealt with; we must reckon with similar evidence of esthetic thinking in other fields. "The first mensuration of time in ornamental elements," says Franz Eppel, "was aimed at by the rhythmic pairing of dots in equidistant repetition on decorated bone staves. The resulting beat—: : : or . . . . . .—is already of a higher sort than the simple linear rhythm that could as well be ascribed to primitive human movements like walking, breathing, or work-motions. The coupling of rhythmic pairs into beats would more probably derive from the dance, and it is no accident that such ornamentation was first invented by Cromagnon man, the creator of plastic art and probably of all those human activities that were later held to be devoted to the Muses."

On the flute with fingerholes the analogy between a visible series of dots and an audible series of tones is "palpable." The mimetic tendencies of those ancient huntsmen, manifested in their imitation of animals, may also have led to their voices carrying out rows of tones in imitation of fixed and clearly separated dots; actually we have evidence of primitive peoples, e.g. in the Congo, imitating flutes and horns. Yet the imitation of instruments should not be overestimated, just as spontaneous grasp of "natural orders" without any instrumental model should not be underestimated. The fact that there are very primitive peoples without instruments, but probably none that sing without any differentiated pitch, speaks for the priority of voice and ear, which were only confirmed by the instrument and sought to produce tonal distinctions the more clearly in accordance with it.

If one compares the music of those peoples of today that correspond to the Stone-Age periods before the art of rock painting flourished, they fall into two groups. In the one, by and large the elder—Australian aborigines, Tasmanians, Vedda of Ceylon, Fuegians and others who are, it is true, partially reprimitivized—singing is habitually stepwise in a narrow vocal range (music ex. 1). Unmistakable consonances hardly occur, and the intervals are not major or minor seconds but imprecise or vascillating distances. But the tones are separated, and more regularly pulsing rhythms are adhered to than transcriptions have heretofore made clear. In a second group of peoples, such as the Papua, Negritos and other Pygmies, the voice very often moves in fanfare-like "triads" (music ex. 2). Both groups realize the two primordial kinds of melody: the former, stepwise intervals, the play around a central tone and differentiation between the raised voice and points of repose—the latter, horizontal consonance and a stationary circling within it.

Fourth, fifth, and octave, those basic elements of musical harmony, came into power even in early prehistoric times. As "natural orders" in the sense of today's *Gestalt* psychology, they early impressed themselves upon consciousness, much as the circle, the angle, and other pregnant forms of the visible world did in Stone-Age ornamentation. They were fundamental to the construction of the oldest scales, like the tetra- and pentatonic (four or five tones within the octave), which certainly did not first appear in script cultures but had long been habitual norms inherent in melody types, and which were employed primarily as a matter of custom, not as abstractly fixed laws. In the simplest orders a fourth or a fifth forms either the frame or the central interval. Thus tens of thousands of years before the Greek tetrachordal system the fourth was filled out by steps which at first, however, and in contrast to the proper tetrachord, were not yet seconds of definite size. That these too became stabilized was probably due in the main to the working together of several consonances. Thus in three- and four-tone melodies—for example, c-f-g-c′—the certainty of the pregnant consonances c-f, c-g, f-c′, and g-c′ brought with it the defining of the step f-g, which now, from being an uncertain distance, became a "whole tone" and acquired the significance of an established interval. It was intended as a definite quantity and incorporated in the rules of the mental game of "music."

On the basis of such factual tonal relationships, comprehensible without theory, notation, and instruments, bi-, tri-, tetra-, and pentatonic systems evidently took form as early as in Paleolithic times. That the last named of these could not have arisen as late as during the Neolithic among settled matriarchal societies is shown by its diffusion among African Pygmies, Eskimo, and other particularly ancient peoples. Heptatonic scales, on the other hand, with distinctions between large and small seconds as well as chromatic structures, probably did first appear in high cultures. That the half-tone-less pentatonic is older than heptatonic modes is evident from the map of its diffusion and rests upon the fact that it is more easily viable than the latter in the absence of theory and schooling.

The comparative prehistory of music confirms the findings of the newer psychology and of systematic musicology: it shows the primality of "natural orders," of a regular rhythmic pulse, of the 4-measure group, of the chief consonances, and of elementary tonal forms. Our musical example 3 illustrates a type of singing practiced by central African Pygmies and other correspondingly primitive peoples. Here we have a woman yodeling in triple time, with leaps within the triad, and she has not learned this from any Alpine farm-wife. Her voice skips up and down among the five tones in fairly pure intervals, which she intends and hits. As it leaps and swings in a regular pulse it carries out a play of sheer equilibrium, harmonically and rhythmically ordered: pure music fullfledged.

Tonality and tonal functions are also practiced among such primitive peoples, if one understands these two terms in the widest sense. Tonality is the building up of tonally related steps with a center of reference; tonal functions are the positional values and roles of tonal steps within a given order and as members of a pattern. If—in an antiphonal rowing-song, for example—to the group's ostinato c-d-f a single voice answers g-f g-f, this reveals a rudimentary functioning of tonic (f) and dominant (c or c-g). These functions appear even more distinctly in melodic formulas like f-d-c—c'-a-g-f.

Finally, elementary forms of polyphony also reach back into prehistory. This is shown by their amazingly wide diffusion among the so-called ancient races, such primitive stock as the Pygmies in Africa and on Malacca, the Bushmen and others (cf. music exx. 30 ff.). Here original forms of reponsorial and choral singing have been preserved, such as stationary circling within a triad, interspersed with shouts and supported by hand-clapping and foot-stamping; such, too, as parallel singing, which the Middle Ages were to carry further as parallel organum; and such, even, as elementary types of drone and canon.

3

FROM THE NEOLITHIC TO
THE IRON AGE

The periods of world history differ greatly in length. Whereas in the story of the earth, we count the great prehistoric periods in millons of years, we divide the history of the Hominids in hundreds of thousands, the Paleolithic era, the older portion of the period of homo sapiens, in tens of thousands, the Meso- and Neolithic at first in millennia and later in centuries, and times since then in even briefer spans. A hastening of tempo and a lessening of the count in years are undeniable. This quickening is certainly not to be attributed to a shortening of perspective. It is a fact that from 80,000 to 8000 in the early Paleolithic no more took place in the history of music than between 500 before and 500 after Christ, or between 1850 and 1950.

The Paleolithic, and with it the bloom of the primitive hunter civilizations, came to an end around 8000 B.C., when after the close of the glacial era the forest began its advance and with the dwindling of the steppe the herds of bison, wild horses, and other big game, hitherto man's partners and source of nourishment, disappeared. Hunting lost its focal position, became incidental or concerned only part of the population, involving as it now did only the meager game of the forest, while fishing, on the other hand, increased. The gathering of fruits became correspondingly more urgent, and this brought woman, upon whom the task of food-gathering had alway devolved, into a more central position. From the Paleolithic through the Mesolithic to the Neolithic the development led from a roving existence of hunting and food-gathering to a settled life based on agriculture, from dependence on the wild offerings of Nature to deliberate cultivation and enclosure. And as man turned to planting, sowing, reaping for his sustenance he changed his way of living. He settled in fixed places and developed a village culture the roots of which still underlie today's peasant-farmer community. In this altered way of life music took on new meaning and new forms.

As the first high civilizations were later to do, the first village cultures appeared in the Near East, notably in Iraq and in Syria. By 6000 Jericho was a city-like settlement surrounded by walls. Houses of men arose, and houses of God. The earliest clay objects yet uncovered—among them terra cotta figures we take to be maternal divinities—date from around 5000; because of these the Neolithic is also known as the Ceramic Age. The new way of life spread from the Near East over Europe, beginning in Central Europe two or three millennia later. It is very important to clarify these connections in order to combat unhistorical conceptions about the origin and age of our own civilization and avoid the tendency to consider as many things as possible indigenous and permanent, as though we must play off the eternal Occident against the eternal Orient—a proceeding not only nationalistic but also anachronistic, for there were no Occident and Orient at that time in terms of the cultures and spiritual attitudes those names bring to mind today. European civilization is not altogther autochthonous, but should be considered within the framework of human history.

In the Neolithic the first farmers' customs came into being, for now life centered around the meaningful cycle of the agricultural year. In these customs, music held an important place. Types of music-making arose that dealt with fertility in plants and in man. Songs, dances, instruments used today in primitive agricultural communities at sowing time and reaping to invoke the magic powers of rain and growth give us an idea of the Neolithic forms and significances from which they have sprung.

A tendency to melodious singing in brief lines with pulsating rhythm seems to be, if not generally typical, at least a characteristic trait in the songs of settled planter peoples. Fifth-century Mesopotamian pottery pictures women's dances: womanhood and motherhood were dominant concepts at that time, although woman's social position was not generally higher in comparison with earlier times and she still bore the chief burden of labor in the fields. In reaction perhaps to her new precedence in these civilizations, the men began to club together, and from the association of ideas of growth and death, earth and the grave, ancestor-worship developed, which presupposes a settled population honoring its dead. In such cults originate dances designed to induce fertility by stamping on an ancestral grave, as well as those mask-dances in which masked men represent the deceased, demanding gifts; quite likely, also, the notion that the ancestor's voice is heard in the bullroarer.

Among the many clay objects of this period were drums, rattles, bells, but other things were made of vegetable material, as for example, stamping tubes of bamboo. Older instruments, like the flute with fingerholes, continued to spread in use and acquired new significance. They must have become increasingly melodic, though we do not know whether the fingerholes were now bored so as to give intended musical intervals. As before, multi-purpose artifacts were used, though not exclusively, for producing sounds. "Many primitive musical instruments (drums, stamping tubes, bows, rattle sticks, bullroarers, scrapers)," says Marius Schneider, "are closely allied to utensils (pots, pestles, weapons, throwing sticks, funeral staves) and serve primarily only to manifest in sound the will to action." The designs on clay skin-headed drums, like the radiant circle and the swastika, are probably in part pure ornament, in part symbolic; Otto Seewald points out that most of these originated in the Near East and reached Central Europe via Southeast Europe. To demonstrate the importance of ethnology for prehistory Behn expressly cites this explanation of Neolithic clay utensils used as hand drums with stretched membranes. Presumably certain artifacts of ancient Egypt and Mesopotamia, heretofore differently interpreted, should be similarly regarded as such drums.

In the Neolithic period civilizations developed that are known as *Megalithic* after the huge stones they dealt with. Originating in mountain regions of southern Asia, they spread to western Europe, from Spain to Ireland and Scandinavia, and in another direction as far as Polynesia. An early stage of Megalithic tombs is represented by the dolmen (c. 3000–2500), a later stage by row-graves or mounds. These structures have been called the cyclopean foundation of man's oldest high cultures, and looked upon as the first architecture to focus on eternity; they served an ancestor-worship of grand style. In the area connected with the tomb of a chief or some other prominent man, dances, ritual dramas, and contests took place; in these and in processions moving on long, broad avenues the fundamental forms of cultic and ceremonial music may well have developed. Many a circle of great stones is set up in relation to the stars, and very likely the earliest ideas associating music with the cosmos go back to these civilizations.

A recent theory suggests that certain arrangements of stones symbolize the representation and perpetuation of ritual dances;

that a central theme stemming from primeval rock-drawings may indeed have been carried over into the high cultures: for objectivization in stone holds fast rites, sacrifices, and prayers vital to the health of the community, lending them permanence and lasting influence. Hence many remains of architectural and plastic art may be interpreted as "frozen music," in the sense not of some speculative esthetic but of cultural history. This question deserves examination independently of those on which it may follow, namely, to what extent specific melodies of medieval Spain and elsewhere may have been, as Schneider assumes, represented by "singing stones."

Schneider also dates back to the later Megalithic that important complex of archaic polyphony the traditions of which spread in a narrow belt from northern and southern Europe across the Caucasus and Afghanistan and further through Indonesia and Melanesia into the South Seas. From this nucleus sprang the polyphony on the one hand of the West and on the other of the Indonesian orchestra. The use of large stones for producing sounds surely stems from these Megalithic cultures. Excavations and traditions show single phonoliths that are set into vibration like bells, as well as rows of lithophones; there has been much argument about these counterparts of the xylophones and serial metallophones and about their tuning. Of Megalithic heritage may also be the sounding stones of China, as well as the singular phenomenon of ancient Egypt's so-called Columns of Memnon—the statues, one broken, of Amenophis (Amenhotep) III—of which Hegel, in his *Aesthetic*, says: "resting, composed in themselves, motionless, arms pressed tight along their bodies, feet close together, fixed, rigid, and lifeless they stand facing the sun, to await the ray that shall touch them, animate them, set them sounding."

Further development took place at one point among primitive peoples through the nomads, roving shepherds, probably an offshoot of planter-civilizations mingled with ancient hunters. Particular historic importance attaches to the bellicose horsemen who by overrunning and subjugation of well-to-do sedentary peoples gave impetus to the formation of higher civilizations. While in their social organization these superior cattle-breeders arrived at a sort of aristocratic hierarchy, they also laid down the corresponding forms for musical activity, thus providing the basis for the further development of music in high cultures. From these peoples come heroic songs and other types of sung epic narrative. Among Asiatic nomads such songs still exist: "In every yurta [nomad hut] the professional singer and poet, who wanders from camp to camp reciting epic tales or songs, is a specially welcome guest. Often he plucks an accompaniment on a stringed instrument." [1]

Continuing developments of such primitive epic song are also met with today among Balkan gusla players in Serbia and elsewhere, among the Finnish Kalevala singers, and in certain backward regions of Europe, while on the script-culture level it was further evolved in the great heroic epic from the *Iliad* to the *Nibelungenlied*.

Traditions inherited from the early pastoral civilizations have been preserved among herder peoples of Asia and Africa, and on the continent of Europe especially among mountain shepherds from the Caucasus to Scandinavia; comparative study of these shows a number of features, some of which in their occidental form were regarded as pastoral in style, to be of ancient heritage. To these belong the *jubili pastorales*, a wordless singing of separate calls or long-spun melodies without rhythmic measure (music ex. 7). Since the time of the prehistoric hunters, shepherd peoples have kept and developed melody in a wide triadic ambit. Cattle and other large animals, often reverenced in ritual, were the theme of dances and songs as well as of the Alpine cowherd's call (the *Kuhreigen* or *ranz des vaches*). Tuneful melody is widespread, particularly among African and Asiatic races; it probably stems from planter culture. It may well have been altered by the shepherd-horsemen to an almost martial swing (music ex. 23b). Memories of ancient times lived on in the pastoral idyl, carried on not only since Theocritus and Virgil in an imaginary Arcadian setting but also in oriental high cultures: the shepherd while guarding his grazing flock plays his flute, communing with the Muses (see also illus. 1).

[1] Ulrich Johansen, in Heinrich Tischner's *Völkerkunde* (1959), p. 113.

Early history was further shaped not only by these warlike herders, but also by migrations and changes taking place among peoples and language groups like the Indo-European, the Celtic, and the Germanic; and particularly also by influences spreading from the higher cultures that meanwhile had come into being, as one may see, for example, by infiltrations of Greek art in the style of the Iron-Age Celts of La Tène, the pole-village in the swamps of Lake Neuchâtel in Switzerland (c. 500 B.C.). In connection with these influences and with the warrior aristocracy of the time the use of metals increased, for which reason the Bronze Age and the Iron Age following upon it are together distinguished from the Stone and the Ceramic Ages as the Metallic Age. Musical instruments too were now made of metal, achieving new character by partaking in this new symbol of power and artistic skill. Animal horns were replaced in the upper classes of society by horns of metal. The lur, that magnificent wind instrument of the Bronze Age in northern Europe, has been found in Denmark, Sweden, and Norway, as well as in North Germany. In appearance and sonority these large S-shaped bronze trumpet-like instruments give expression to the sense of brilliant clarity that was a dominating feature of the period. The ideal of a tense, proud bearing, reflected in the clothes and armor of the time, too, may well have affected the rhythm and melody of the music.

Research into early European times is one of the rewarding tasks of musicology seeking as it does the history of music not only in the West but in the entire continent. Sources are provided in the first place by pictures and instruments (horns, lyres, pan-pipes, etc.). The pictures show, for example, cultic round-dances and lur-blowing during sacrifices held on sacred ships of the Bronze Age, as well as a sacrificial scene, music performed for dining, and Celtic horn and trumpet players of the Iron Age. Secondly, we have reports concerning heroic songs and songs of praise, the playing of harp and kithara, the various activities of which music was a part: a Frankish wedding, for example, a Hunnish banquet, a Gothic funeral lament. These we know of through ecclesiastical interdictions of pagan customs. In a martyrology telling of the murder of three missionaries in the mountain valley of Nonsberg in the southern Tyrol (in 397 A.D.), there is mention of the tuba (perhaps a bark trumpet of alphorn type) which, loud and strong, was to drive evil away, call the people together for worship, and excite the warriors to combat. There is also mention of the tintinnabulum (bell or jingle), which had magic significance not only for sheep-herding. Ritual song is described as strident and frightening: *strepentes et horridi jubili pastorales* sound while a ritual punishment is carried out, the burning of one of the missionaries who had opposed pagan rites; this would surely not have been yodeling but another sort of those jubilations that once not only expressed overflowing joy but also had numinous and magic meaning. Furthermore, later customs seem to be survivals of archaic ones, as, for example, the account of the round-dance performed by young people on Christmas Eve of the year 1020 in the cemetery of the Anhalt village of Kölbigk. With this musical round-dance they were going through the motions of a wedding, carrying out the nuptial course according to ancient custom on the burial ground of their ancestors.

Linguistics also cast some light upon music. For example, the singing and calling with few or no words, known in Latin as *jubilus*, evidently stems from early times. Authors of Antiquity and early Christendom ascribe it to the pagan countryfolk. Saint Hilarius of Poitiers (d. 367) speaks of *jubilus pastoralis agrestique*, and Saint Augustine (d. 430) says: *Maxime jubilant qui aliquid in agris operantur* (Especially those who work in the fields sing jubili). The Latin word belongs to a widespread word family linked with the exclamations "io" and "yu": Greek ἰύζω (*yudzo*, cry out), Latin *jubilo*, Serbian *yuju*, German *Juchhe*, *jauchzen*, *juchzen*, *jodeln*, *johlen*, etc., English "hoho!," "yoohoo!" and so forth. "Yo" and "yu" were exclamations not only of joy but also of surprise and of pain. It is a mistake to impute to *jubilare* the sense of jubilation that first came into it in the Middle Ages through mixture with a Hebrew expression deriving from a musical instrument, the *jobel*, and leading to words like jubilee, jubilary. Nor is it to be translated simply as yodeling, which is only one of the types of wordless singing or calling designated by this word-family; it differs from other types in constantly changing vocal registers.

Legends and fairy tales inform us of the former significance of music. They show how belief in its magic powers persisted from prehistoric times. In folk tales of the Finns, the Finno-Ugrian Cheremisses of Eastern Russia, Italians, Africans, and others, instruments like the flute, the horn, the harp exert their magic power; they call to animals, entice and help to capture them.[2] This is the same theme as in the Stone-Age picture referred to earlier (illus. 2a).

But the most fruitful method for finding out about music of primitive times in the European area and laying bare the roots of medieval Western music is the comparative study of three main treasuries of melodic material: 1) folklore traditions in widely separated parts of our hemisphere, from the Balkans to Iceland, from Spain to Finland; 2) sacred and secular songs in medieval notation: old strata of Gregorian chant, refrains of convivial songs since the troubadours and trouvères, and so forth; 3) extra-European music, particularly of peoples with Eurasian and Eurafrican associations (Ob-Ugrian tribes, Kirghiz, Mongols, *et al.*). By combining these sources it has been possible to show that certain formula-types—the models, for example, upon which epic songs were sung (music ex. 8)—antedate the Middle Ages. It further appears that the melodies of popular sacred songs, like those of the Flagellants written down in the 14th century or the Easter song *Christ ist erstanden* ("Christ is risen"), stem from melodic types that from their nature and their diffusion must be considerably older. By and large, pre-pentatonic and pentatonic types, familiar from European nursery songs and songs accompanying social customs, are also found among primitive peoples. Their common traits are not altogether to be explained by polygenetic origin of such simple forms in different, totally independent corners of the globe; but certain types bear a family relationship in the historical sense of the term, stemming from the same archaic roots.

[2] Cf. Stith Thompson, *Motif-Index of Folk Literature*, D. 1441 (and elsewhere).

ESSENTIAL CHARACTERISTICS OF EARLIEST MUSIC SURVIVING AMONG PRIMITIVE PEOPLES

An extensive heritage from earliest times is to be found among primitive peoples of today. Many traits of their styles therefore represent essential features of music in the First Age. Of these only a few will be pointed out here, supplementing the foregoing sections of this chapter.

Music was originally linked with the life of a community and for the most part functioned not in a specific musical group but, for example, throughout a whole village. Still far ahead lay the days when the world of this art would be represented by patrons, connoisseurs, and amateurs, or lone composers with their partisans. Yet in early times there already was individual possession and even a sort of copyright, which reserved to an author the use of his own song; he could cede it to another against compensation, otherwise no one else might sing his melody, which to this extent was no folksong. In this respect as in others the First Age of music history is not to be roughly summed up in simplistic terms; there was opposition then too between individual and community.

Certain individuals stood out above the average: singers and instrumentalists, inventors of new tunes, leaders of rites and other ceremonies. To prove themselves in song contests, like those still held among Eskimos and pastoral peoples, they were obliged to practice and improve their performance, and for this hunters and shepherds had plenty of time. That the gods set effort before fame holds good in all times; we see from various sketches that have been preserved how the Stone-Age artists of the rock pictures had to experiment and learn before they could achieve their works. Music belonged to the sorcerer's profession and later to that of the medicine man or the shaman. Other members of the tribe habitually took over regular musical functions of instrumentalists or leader of song; but professional musicians, who lived entirely or in large part by their music, appeared only later, in differentiated societies.

Though this early music was not based on explicit theory and notation, it had its order and its playing rules. Performance of cultic songs on which the welfare of the community seemed to hang often clung to a rigorous exactitude. Musical works of art, compositions as we know them, there were none, only types, models, ways of singing to be followed. Melodies were more or less variable, but divergences were held within bounds by community control so that long preservation was possible. For the most part the only form in primitive music lies in short lines to be sung or played; these were repeated many times, with variants, without there being any set over-all structure. A chain of 30 or 33 variants does not imply any architectonic form, as do the variation cycles of a Bach or Beethoven, yet in an epic song or in the course of a rite with many parts a sense of musical form could come through. One principle of quite elementary form is intensification, gradual at first and increasing in speed to the end.

Music played a far greater part in the central realities of life than it did later. "It wove," says Herder, "about present objects, actions, events, about a living world." It was an element in work, war, healing, judgment, whether performed during these activities or in ritual preparation and accomplishment—for example in hunting-spells. By its very nature music lends itself to the working of magic. Its effects were surely not limited to esthetic enchantment or to invoking protection or fertility, a scheme into which some authors try to fit everything. The historian must not only record, but understand. Young Herder warns of this, and indeed, specifically with regard to the meaning and influence of primitive music. "There are dark spots in the history of nations and of the human spirit in various times, upon which light can be cast only through a certain knowledge of psychology. Thus it is with the music of the peoples who had bound fast its tones to certain ideas and its accents to certain subjects; who possessed their songs of war and of concord, their tones of anger and of love, their melodies of wisdom and of vice. We would of course find some exaggerations in these. . . . But in a pragmatic history of music we would, before judging, try to understand, and perhaps say: 'See there! a rough, simple, but deeply feeling people.'" Herder is reckoning with effects of the art of the Muses that were once recognized but "the possibility of which in illness and hypertension we hardly grasp today."

We should also remember that after 1600 there were trends in music that sought to accomplish psychic effects similar to those made famous by the myths of Antiquity. Like the fairy operas of the Romantic period, sorcerers and shamans on their elementary level symbolized the supernatural by using low and high registers beyond the normal range of the human voice, driving it to extremes from whispering to yelling, with repetition in growing excitement and intensity to the point of ecstasy. Thus the magic of music was linked with that of word, mask, and intoxicating movement. Little as all this expenditure of effort on the imaginary domination over nature could make up for the lack of real domination over external forces by technical means, not to be achieved until the Fourth Age of our history, such real effects were nevertheless brought about by psycho-physical suggestion—in medicine, for example—so that belief in the magic power of music could persist and assert itself. Because of the effects an individual felt in himself, he could believe that with this rhythmic sound he possessed "the innermost strength of a creature" and therewith could achieve domination over it, or through analogous rhythms "set in motion," as Marius Schneider puts it, "the stagnating fundamental forces of the world."

Music not only had a humanizing influence, but also served the contrary inclination that dwells in man's nature: the need to alienate himself, transform himself into some demonic being and give himself over to the strange fantasy world of the soul. As

masks did, particularly voice-masks, certain analogous tones in-
duced an often highly intensive state of ecstasy, even though the
theatrical miming of an animal, an ancestor, a demon, can itself
also sharpen the conscious distinction between imitator and im-
itated; in this, different types of people evidently acted differently.
We have many reports of how shamans artifically induce their
ecstasies through music and other means. According to Johansen [3]
"the shaman is able to put himself, mostly with the aid of a drum
he beats, into trances during which he can send his soul journey-
ing to those other worlds that exist beside our own, and compel
various spirits to his service."

In all this, primal experience and tradition, custom and mythos
work together. When a Polynesian tale tells of a magic song at-
tracting fish that are later transformed into half-human dancers,
the myth is based on the custom of using animal masks as, inversely, the custom derives its significance from the myth. Nor
does this whole interrelation of imagination and representation
always expend itself in magic and ecstasy; religious actions and
emotions are no less vital. Like the later art of music, primitive
music touches the numinous quality that embraces power, awful-
ness, and fascination. To many peoples the bullroarer was the
voice of an ancestor, but the full experiencing of its effect could
include more than a simple connection with the deceased; it took
on numinous significance when in initiation rites the boys were
led into the forest at night to be inducted into the sacred traditions
of the tribe through its whizzing roar. Music with its penetrating
power that represents no particular objects or persons, fitted
especially well into the dynamistic concept of the world, which
interpreted the divine force as impersonal "mana."

Besides religious and magic-working music primitive societies
too have secular music, songs gay or humorous, for mockery or
ridicule, as among the Eskimo, or the interminable recitation of
trivial incidents, as among the Pygmies. Applicable to music also
is the view—a view newly confirmed by ethnology today after a
period that held exaggerated notions of the differences between

[3] *Op. cit.,* p. 162.

peoples—that the whole human race widely conforms in intellectual and spiritual as well as in physical characteristics. Schneider rightly emphasizes this universal coherence and points to the ancient symbol of the tree representing growth. "Manifold as are the roots of music, its trunk nevertheless reveals a series of traits common to all peoples. Upon what else should the universally understandable part of music rest? Only with the unfolding of its branches do particularities, geographical, historical, cultural, again begin to differ."

Variety in unity arises from differences between races and peoples in their psychic tempo, their models of behavior, their habits of movement, as well as from the diversity and variously broad diffusion of cultural elements, not to mention changing times and geographical situations. Today's primitive folk have preserved their heritage from prehistoric and early times selectively and altered it variously. Here it has been carried further with innovations, there dried and become encrusted or again regressed to the archaic. These processes are clearly shown by their instruments. These have been adorned with ornaments and symbols not only to enrich their appearance but to enhance their power and effectiveness—slit drums, for example, carved and decorated with idols. As we have seen, utensils previously made of plant or animal materials available in a natural environment came to be made of metal, like bells and bronze drums. Increase in size to the gigantic—met with in other things among savage and rural peoples—led to man-sized drums and even larger forms known to measure 20 feet in length and 6 in breadth. Gigantic flutes and bark trumpets or alphorns run up to 12 feet in length. Another development of simple instrumental types is the lining up or bundling together of staves, slabs, pipes to form scaled instruments such as the xylophone, lithophone, and panpipes.

All along the line, however, one must also take account of the strong influences radiating from the high cultures of Antiquity and later from Islam. Owing to these, great differences came about between, for example, those African tribes far removed geographically and psychologically from high-culture areas, like

Pygmies and Bushmen, and the kingdoms of northern Africa. Yet even these influences, as we shall presently see, cannot compare in strength to the overpowering floods of music spreading everywhere today thanks to industry and technique.

 **II**

THE SECOND AGE

MUSIC IN THE HIGH CIVILIZATIONS
OF ANTIQUITY AND THE ORIENT

THE EARLY HIGH CIVILIZATIONS

The first societies to pass beyond the confines of the primitive through writing, the building of cities, the organization of the state, and other features essential to higher civilization came into being around 3000 B.C.; these were the Sumerian and the Egyptian. Of the approximately contemporary Indus civilization very little has been preserved, very little discovered, while the Chinese, which because of its legendary heritage has been looked upon as particularly old, in reality did not begin until later.

Certain characteristics of high cultures had become apparent earlier but they came to full development only by the putting forth of extraordinary efforts. Both Mesopotamia and Egypt were compelled to overcome great difficulties of a physical nature arising from existence beside violent great rivers, the fertilizing effect of whose floods called for a communal exploitation which also brought about a more intensive organization of life. The theocratic states that grew up at that time centered in the cult. And in this, music too took on new functions.

Mesopotamia

The Sumerian civilization centered more closely than almost any other on religion, and music was so compactly interwoven with it that from the sources known some scholars assume there had been no secular singing and playing at all in those days. In the hands of priests and professional musicians, music played a role in festivities, on important occasions, and especially in daily temple services. Many of the hymns and prayers of which the texts have been preserved were sung to the harp, the lyre, or some other instrument; their titles specifically indicate this: "Flute Lament for Enlil," "Song with Accompaniment of the Lyre," "Timbrel Song."

The many reproductions of sculptures assembled by André Parrot in his great book *Sumer* (published in 1960) give a rich picture of the religious world in which this oldest temple or "church" music took part and from which it must have derived its meaning and its character. We see praying figures in postures familiar to us from the Catholic Church: on their knees, hands folded, faces filled with awe and humility. We meet types of priests and high priests who also remind us of the church and of our Middle Ages, and find familiar religious themes like the Good Shepherd and the Divine Mother and Child. In forms of piety and representations of divinity the Sumerians laid foundations that still endure in the Christian Church and in other religions. Presumably the archaic groundwork of liturgical song surviving in Jewish, Christian, and other services also goes back to them.

The monumental temples of the Sumerians were images of the cosmos. They were praised in many songs. Inner connections between divine house and divine service, and hence between temple and music, were here expressed. Ritual music accompanied the building or repairing of these structures. The musical instruments that sounded while the priest-king Gudea (3rd century B.C.) laid the cornerstone and himself fashioned the first tile, were the same that played later in the court before the finished temple. A hymn on the temple of En-Ki E'engurra in "the good city" of Eridu in South Babylonia includes these verses:

> "Thy call pours forth like that of a broad high-flowing
>   river to King En-Ki:
>
> For his sacred house he prepares all things well.
> Lyres, algar-instruments, harps, timbrels,

sistra, instruments from Sabum and Ma'eri, that fill the house;
sweet tones, the voice of the harp,
are made to sound amid his terrible splendor,
the algar-instrument sacred to En-Ki sounds for him amid
    his terrible splendor,
all the musicians play for him.
En-Ki's word is not to be overthrown,
it is set for the days of eternity."
Thus spake Isimu to the walls being built,
praised the house E'engurra in the sweet song.
When it was built, when it was built,
when En-Ki's Eridu had been raised high,
it was like a strong stepped mountain rooted beside the water.

The intimate connection between temple building and temple music lasted beyond the Sumerian period. A Babylonian-Assyrian ritual for laying the cornerstone of a temple prescribes what is to be sung at the various ceremonies: "The cantor sings 'to destroy the masonry walls' . . . ; after which he sings 'Prince, reconcile yourself,' 'Shamash is king,' and 'Through the lament of comforting the heart' to timbrel accompaniment . . . [and later] at the bricklaying, 'When Anu created the heavens.' " Prescriptions such as this point to a feature fundamental in the history of cult music: the order of the songs and their place in the liturgy, as later in the "church year." In her dissertation on Sumerian cult music Henrike Hartmann points out how the distinction between songs of praise and songs of lament was carried out. According to the time of year, either no laments or, on the other hand, no hymns of praise or their accompanying instruments, were to be heard. Falkenstein and von Soden, in their collection of *Sumerian and Accadian Hymns and Prayers*, speak of these song-types and assume that their classification relates to certain styles of musical execution; the indications "Songs to the Lyre" and "Timbrel Song" are to be thus understood. "Anyone who knew the old cult rules would easily be able to deduce from the superscription into what cultic frame the song was intended to fit."

It is clear from the song texts as well as from pictures and directions in what rites music took part and what ideal meaning it must accordingly convey. Libations were offered to the deity on sacred platters, to the playing of the lyre or the harp. Music had a part in processions, in the cult of the dead, in unusual events, like rites to dispel the evil consequences of a lunar eclipse. One ritual for the last-named occasion prescribes "the plucking of strings all day long." At ritual feasts drums and timbrels sounded to merry tunes. "The countries rejoice at thy pure cults . . . ," says an Accadian prayer to Ishtar. "The Prince, who fears thee, offers thee the cults thou didst desire. May the masters of the cults celebrate in joyful festivity; may their hearts be glad at the music." And for an example of quite opposite character there are these verses from an ancient Babylonian prayer at the viewing of a nocturnal sacrifice: "The night is veiled,/ the palace lies numb,/ all silent are the steppes; whoever is still upon his way, calls on the god."

At banquets, ceremonies sacred and profane intermingled, as in later Antiquity and in early Christendom before the Last Supper became a spiritualized concept. Sumerian celebrations of the New Year, of victories, of feasts after battle—as they are shown in a pictorial account, in which both a singer and a lyre-player also take part—are similarly undifferentiated. The same may be said of popular festivals and hymns to the goddess Ishtar, who may be compared to the Egyptian goddess Hathor: "The citizens of Kishi, they dance with sistra in their left hands; the center of the town is full of the sound of timbrels; outside, pipes and drums re-echo."

Music with no relation to cult is referred to in a prayer to Nergal, god of the underworld, that he may spare those who enjoy life, innocent and playful: "Lord, do not go to the playground, do not drive the children from the playground; there where stringed instruments sound do not enter; the young singer who knows his music, do not drive him away!" Music other than cultic is also attested to by genre scenes of a later time, in one of which drums and cymbals accompany a boxing match.

Still from the first half of the third millennium come illustrations of music-making animals; the themes may well be taken from familiar myths or legends. An inlay on a lyre from Ur also shows the mythical tamer of wild animals, perhaps to be identified with Gilgamesh, as well as half-animal creatures. These motifs must stem from ancient traditions rooted in pretotemic belief and miming dances with animal masks (cf. p. 22 above and illus. 2a). Later this tradition led in Europe to music-making animals on romanesque capitals, in the medieval *Roman de Fauvel,* and in the tale of the town musicians of Bremen. According to their content also the Sumerian pictures are presumably to be interpreted as an intermediate form: mythical subjects with fairytale features, half serious, half jestingly grotesque. Ancient animal-miming figures continued to live on in a lower sphere than that of the new high world of gods, as the half-animal satyrs and sirens did in Greek mythology.

The connection of music with mythical animals also appears in the costly lyres and harps decorated with bulls' heads in gold, silver, or precious stones, and here the creature, as in Egypt and Crete, must have been symbolic of higher religion. In the building of instruments as in so many other things, the Sumerians made a truly fundamental contribution. According to Behn, "the instruments sooner or later taken over in European music from the classical civilizations of the Mediterranean countries are in large part descended from the ancient Mesopotamian culture centers." Central to the Sumerian cult stood the lyre, and next it the harp. In Gudea's time large round drums were among the principal temple instruments. Small hand drums, played by women, we know of from the earliest periods of Sumerian culture and they surely derive from a Neolithic tradition. If a few instruments were honored as sacred ritual objects, it is also to be remembered that the Sumerians distinguished their types of religious poetry according to the instruments to which they were sung. Singing "to" an instrument, in effectively planned concurrence, seems not to have been achieved until in early high civilizations. Evidently the playing of an instrument was of great significance in the development of poetry, particularly lyric poetry—greater perhaps than has heretofore been realized.

Beside the Egyptians, the Sumerians were the first to develop a fully organized musical profession and to have pictured prototypes of musicians, like the female singer and the harpist. Ritual music was executed by musicians of priestly rank, beside whom women also functioned in similar capacities. Function and rank had specific names; the former often passed from father to son but could also be purchased. Cuneiform lists mention several musicians by name. In certain royal tombs musicians both male and female are buried with their master; belief in a future life in the nether world demanded that they, like others of the royal retinue, accompany the king in death.

Fundamental to the history of cultic song were, finally, certain types of form that derive from Sumerian poetry or were first transmitted through it. Here we already have the *parallelismus membrorum* familiar to us from the Psalms, a construction in paired verses of similar content. Psalm-like verses alternate with refrains, as in the Christian chant; presumably the verse was sung by a cantor, the refrain by a group, as in the ancient Jewish cult. The text provides places for ritual obeisance that act also as articulating pauses, and were perhaps linked with instrumental interludes. One of these form-types is called "Long Song," although the texts to most of the examples preserved are short, and as Falkenstein and von Soden have noted, in none of them is any formal articulation indicated. Perhaps the name refers to a melismatic solo song. In addition to successions of verses and various forms of litany there are strophic arrangements of equal or unequal numbers of lines. In a long hymn linked together by ten obeisances, the section after the second bow is the following song with three strophes of the same pattern and similar wording:

> They strike for her the sacred algar-instrument—
> stand forth before holy Inanna.
> The great queen of the heavens Inanna I would greet!
>
> They strike the sacred drum for her, the sacred timbrel—
> stand forth before holy Inanna.
> The great queen of the heavens Inanna I would greet!
>
> They strike for her the sacred lyre, the sacred timbrel—
> stand forth before holy Inanna.
> The great daughter of Su'en Inanna I would greet!

A large part of the grandiose culture of the Sumerians was preserved by the peoples who conquered and subjected them.

Cuneiform writing, which the Sumerians developed, was taken over by most Near-Eastern civilizations and their language cultivated as ritual language, as Latin was to be in the Catholic Church. The Assyrians, who dominated Mesopotamia from about 1250 to 612, typify a civilization not original but grafted on that of the conquered, and secularized in comparison with the Sumerian. That music played a part in this secularization is attested by pictures; one, for example, in which Assurbanipal and his Queen are being entertained by harp-playing in the garden, or another showing types of virtuoso instrumentalists and singers, where one of the latter supports the vibrating of his larynx with his hand. Characteristic for the Assyrian military state would be the representation of a trumpeter from Nineveh, and for the international quality of this empire, the picture of the Elamite court choristers taken over, like the choirs of other conquered peoples, by the victorious Assyrians to enhance the glory of their court, their city, their empire. So too, as we know from Psalm 137, in a later day the citizens of Babylon commanded captive Jews to sing them a song of Zion.

Egypt

While the civilization of the Sumerians has been brought to light by research only in the last several decades, and something of its musical side not until recently, the sources for Egyptian culture and its music have been much longer known. Music historians were already dealing with them in the 18th century, and composers—Verdi, above all, in *Aïda*—have long exercised their imagination in picturing the colorful sonorities of the Pharaonic era. Yet our knowledge of this subject has increased considerably in more recent years. Especially thanks to Hans Hickmann we now have a far richer picture of the musicians, the instruments, the chironomy, and other aspects of music in that country.

Of all the high civilizations before classical Antiquity Egypt provides the most sources. Its plastic and pictorial arts, furthermore, cover a wealth of lively subjects realistically pictured.

They clearly show types of the musicians of the time, like the dignified leader of the choir, the blind harpist, the charming young girl at court. They let one sense the music immanent in dance and gesture, and moreover they fix certain procedures in the making of music: lending permanence to the moment, they even give manual signs and positions of the hand on an instrument exactly, thus indirectly enabling us to identify the tones intended by the hand-signs and the combinations of tones being taken by the players on their instruments.

The world of Egyptian life, in which music played a part, resembled in its essential features the Sumerian: sacred royalty and the primacy of the well-organized cult, urban civilization and monumental architecture. Yet differences with Mesopotamia also became operative: the greater isolation of this "oasis civilization" between desert and sea, the uncommon stability of the dominant population (whereas in Mesopotamia Sumerians, Accadians, Assyrians succeeded each other), and the traits of character of this people molded by both Africa and the Mediterranean, which was able to combine the cult of the dead with an abounding vitality, and mathematical abstraction, as in the form of the pyramids, with a more natural and supple expressiveness, as in genre pictures and portraits.

A distinctive feature of Egyptian religious worship, especially in the later period, was its insistence on silence in the presence of the deity. Thus a divine decree concerning the Abaton, the area sacred to Osiris opposite the island of Philae, says: "One may not beat the hand timbrel there nor sing to the harp or the flute. . . . And no one may speak loud . . . during the holy time of the days Isis, Queen of Philae, spends there upon her throne."

But beside the times and the places where silence was to be maintained, there were here as in other civilizations periods when loud rejoicing held sway, much as the darkness in the temple's Holy of Holies contrasted with worship of the sun. The little hymn to Aton of Akh-en-Aton's time celebrates the sun: "Life revives as soon as you have sent your rays, and every land delights in festivity. Singers, musicians, shouters are filled with joy." As in the Accadian prayer to Ishtar, fecund, productive life is celebrated in a hymn to Hathor: "We rejoice before thy countenance, thou Sovereign at Denderah . . . Thou art the queen of jubilation, sovereign of the dance; queen of music-making, sovereign of song; queen of leaping, sovereign of wreath-winding . . . Come ye with jubilation and strike the timbrel day and night! The men drum, the women are full of gaiety."

Another song, also transmitted from Egypt's Greco-Roman times, praises the goddess Hathor as "lovely verdant one, queen of greenness, queen of bright verdancy." In this goddess of love and also of music the moving principle of blooming and growth, of *natura naturans*, was honored. The whole world is said to be animated and beautified through her and thus to tell of her: "Heaven and its gods make music to thee, sun and moon praise thee, the gods and the goddesses honor thee . . . The whole earth makes music for thee, all heaven dances joyfully for thee, all countries and foreign lands honor thee even to the four corners of heaven." These verses remind one of early Christian ideas of the world being filled with the glory and reflected light of God: *Pleni sunt coeli et terra gloria tua.* They also interpret the idea of *musica mundana* (harmony in the macrocosmos), later often thought of merely as numerically conceived, in a more lively and dynamic fashion.

Music filled the world in general and the temple as the symbol of the world. Like incense, which was called "divinizing," it filled the holy places with a sacred fluid during religious ceremonies. Pictures show, beside the priest performing the incense rite before the sacrificial altar, musicians with lyres, harps, and flutes. When the god Ammon appeared in his temple a great harp sounded the praises of his glory; blind harpers are often represented before images of gods. Trumpets gave the signal for greeting the approaching sun and resounded in the presence of the god. But instruments were played especially at festivities and in processions. In a picture cycle from the New Empire the procession is led by a soldier blowing a trumpet, and later come singers and timbrel players; in a long train on the bank, accompanying the sacred ships that bear the god Ammon Re together with the king and queen to Luxor, a group of priests and women sings to the clatter of the sistra, and later dancing and leaping Negroes appear in the cortege.

In archaic religions ritual dance belonged not only to the lively processions of the populace but also to the aristocratic cult. As King David danced before the Ark of the Covenant so also the Pharaoh danced.[1] Even group dances of an acrobatic character were an element in the cult, and as in primitive times ritual round dances were performed at burials and funeral ceremonies. Thus, in custom as in creed, life and death were variously linked.

Music pertained to festive banquets, a treat for the ears. An inscription on a banquetting scene lists joys and delights that together make up a menu, a counterpart to the combination of all arts in the *Gesamtkunstwerk* or the pantomime of Antiquity: "To rejoice in seeing everything beautiful; in singing, dancing, and jubilation; to anoint oneself with myrrh and rub oneself with oil, to inhale the fragrance of the lotus blossom. . . ." The banquet, symbol and substance of well-being and the good life, was to be desired for the dead also, and for oneself after death: music at banquets is often pictured on tombs.

Genre pictures show that singing, instruments, and rhythmic sounds accompanied work: in pasture, at harvest and vintage, litter-bearing and so forth. Here, as in a picture of a choir of blind singers at the temple, both country and city folk are represented; but for the most part the subjects depicted in the arts are the priests and such musicians as were active in the higher cult and the ruling society. Names and dates of musicians have been transmitted even more fully in Egypt than in Mesopotamia. At the head of the hierarchy or social pyramid stood the court conductor, the "overseer of the King's singers and director of pleasures" (as a grave-inscription calls the ancestor of a whole dynasty of musicians), followed by other priests and court musicians. Other dignitaries also had singers and instrumentalists in their service, or persons otherwise employed by them took over musical functions as well; for example, the oldest music-making

---

[1] "The Sacrificial Dance of the Egyptian Kings" is the subject of a dissertation by Herman Kees, Munich, 1912.

Egyptian we know by name was steward of a household around 2700; he is pictured with a drum. Blind harpers took part both at banquets and in cult ceremonies. In the Old Kingdom they had still accompanied the royal family's rites on harps bearing an effigy of the king's head. In these later times they were more rarely called upon for important feasts: they are too dirty and gluttonous, says one text.

On the way from the Neolithic to the high civilizations 4th-millennium vases portray the female dancer. We know of a royal ballet-mistress as early as the Fourth Dynasty, that is, before 2563, and around 2500 of the official title "teacher of the royal (women) singers." Further we have pictures from the Old and Middle Kingdoms of women dancers and singers (cf. illus. 5a). Women also took part in religious services as priestesses. The assumption that they first appeared in the musical life of the New Empire and that theretofore only oriental slaves had set the tone, does not hold good. Countless pictures evidence not those traits which recent writings have characterized as "lascivious" and "orgiastically provocative," but rather models of feminine charm. In the way these girls hold harp or lute in serene elegance, such pictures tell not just of music being made, but of music incarnate. The balance of rhythm and harmony in their tones prompts the movements of the bodies, music is an inner dance guiding and flowing through these slender silhouettes. Here we see how live was the idea of *musica humana* (harmony in the microcosmos, i.e. man) in Antiquity. Thus Richard Hamann speaks of "the scene of the dancing and harp-playing women, who stand there, graceful and yet limp, uncertain, wavering almost, as they rock in their dance, themselves an adornment of life, in gesture and in contours a floating, dissolving music."

For all its abundant vitality, Egyptian civilization was ruled by a strong sense of law and discipline, the idea of order in world, cult, and state which was characterized by the focal word *"maat."* In music too this idea must have had its effect, in the sense rather of practical organization and conduct than of those cosmological speculations that first came to permeate the later phases of Antiquity. The duties and offices of musicians in cult and at court were laid down by the state. "Royal teachers of music" and other pedagogues were charged with the education of priests, professional musicians, and amateurs of music. An "overseer of beautiful girls" and priest of Hathor had himself portrayed instructing the girls of the harem in singing, hand-clapping, and playing the sistrum. Another picture, which looks like a doll's house, shows members of a Pharaonic ladies' ensemble making music in the various rooms of their conservatory. In one room a quartet is practicing harp, lyre, lute, and flute, in another a dancer, a flutist, and a harpist are at work. Striking in the representations of group dancing and group music-making are discipline and balance; they predicate a corresponding precision in the giving of signs, in the simultaneity of performance. Considering the sophistication of the sometimes acrobatic dances and the high level of civilization in general, it is to be assumed that these people were not content with the most elementary rhythms; surviving traditions, indeed, bear this out.

The Egyptian bent for law and order is conclusively expressed in their chironomy. As our illustration 5 shows, it was customary while singing to make signs with the hand which the instrumentalist closely observed. Evidently he followed these indications as we today carry out the composer's indications from written notes. Hickmann has compared various pictures of such hand gestures with each other and with those still used in Coptic ritual singing. In this way he has been able to demonstrate that certain signs of arm and hand stood for certain rhythms and tones. For example, the gesture in which thumb and forefinger form an ◯ seems to represent the tonic, the hand outstretched the recitation tone above this, and a sign with both hands the fifth as a vertical interval. As in early notations, this gesture language probably indicated only the important tones. Evidently the singer knew the melodies, particularly the cult tunes, better than his instrumentalist partner. In any case, he did not take his pitch from the latter but showed him what he had to play. Singer directed instrumentalist.

As "chironomist" he represented law, the norm. What he conveyed with his gesture language was the ideal image or rule hovering above the actual sonorities. When the Egyptians spoke of "singing with the hand" and symbolized this in hieroglyph by an arm, they undoubtedly meant not any singing whatever, as of peasants or Negroes, but only singing as an art that included conducting and notation by gesture.

It will also be possible to draw further conclusions about the music of the Egyptians if one follows Curt Sachs in comparative study of such instruments as have been preserved. They clearly give evidence of historic change. Strong influences from the East brought into the Middle Kingdom and the New Empire various instruments—such as the lyre, the lute, the shrill double oboe—and corresponding styles of instrumental music. Music now became more colorful and varied, more animated, more agitated. But this alteration should not lead to the assumption that the indigenous music of the Egyptians had on the whole been quiet and dignified, losing its original character through invasion from the Orient. Investigations conducted with a better sense of history will, instead of setting up blocklike contrasts between Egypt and the Orient, ascertain specific differences between them and attempt to fathom, beside the constant national factors, the still more important currents of time and events that spread over wide areas. Even in the Near East music had not been "orgiastic" from its beginnings and altogether, but had undergone alterations in the course of time.

Traits Common to the Music of Early High Civilizations

Beside the Mesopotamian and the Egyptian, other civilizations should be taken into account, particularly the Hittite, the Phoenician, and the Minoan. None of these can be summed up in a simple formula; it is hardly fair to think the music of the Syrians was nothing more than "lush and licentious." Furthermore these civilizations did not live each isolated from its neighbors but were so linked through international concerns and so related in essential features that for a brief view in terms of universal history their common traits may prove to be more important than their differences.

The innovations, like writing and urban living, that made for high civilizations, spread later to the Far East and via Greece to Western Europe, but at first they remained limited to the Near East and the eastern Mediterranean. In this area of the Ancient World, while there were strong factors, like pathless and unsafe stretches of country, making for separation, others equally strong made for unity. Wandering musicians, like peddlers, traveled the seas and the roads of empire from country to country. Whole cultures were transplanted by the march of armies and migration of peoples; many a conquered nation's orchestra was taken over into the victor's own court household. Musicians as well as music-making slave-girls provided part of the tribute to be paid or the dowry given, for example, with a daughter of the Pharaoh when she became the wife of Solomon. In addition, central courts and cities set the pattern for others, much as Versailles was to do later in Europe.

Pictures and sculptures accordingly show everywhere the same instruments and instrumental combinations: lyre and harp, for example, with double oboe and frame drum, or a stringed instrument with double-reed pipes and cymbals. The names of the instruments, too, were largely taken over into other languages, and surely not a little of the style of their music came along with them. Herodotus bears witness to the international diffusion of a song among Egyptians, Phoenicians, Greeks, and others. Curt Sachs probably goes too far in concluding from such testimony that the Ancient World possessed its musical language essentially in common and that the music of each individual nation was no more than a dialect. Between Mesopotamia and Egypt in the third millennium there were obviously substantial differences; also, the relation between community and diversity changed, and like the later Greeks, the Cretans of an earlier time, for example, seem to have imprinted upon their music as upon their entire culture a character that went well beyond the peculiarities of any dialect. The fact remains undisputed, however, that international connections were far-reaching.

The special nature of this community of cultures is characterized not so much by the term "Ancient Orient" as by that of "Archaic High Civilizations." For if one interprets "Orient" geographically, one should remember that this cultural area included not only parts of the Near East but parts of Africa and Europe as well; the purely geographical concept does not meet the case. If, however, one understands "Orient" in the sense this word later took on, as counterpart to the Occident, thus including the implication of something foreign, exotic, un-European, one commits an anachronism and fails to overcome the false alternative implying either that ancient Greek music must have had to maintain its indigenous occidental nature against foreign oriental conquest or itself have been at bottom only a provincial facet of the ancient oriental art. Yet in reality the geographic and ethnic differences are of secondary importance; of greater historical significance were the development of preclassical high cultures that took place in that easterly region, as well as the spread and further evolution of these new forms of human existence eastward in Asia and westward in Europe. Of the special nature of its continuation in ancient America we shall not attempt to speak here.

Among the nations of that Ancient World some rose earlier, some later, to high civilization. Thus while the Jews of the Patriarchal time took over elements of high culture from Mesopotamian and Egyptian civilization, generally speaking they had themselves already started on the way to creating a full high culture. But if writing and written works are essential to the concept of "high culture," how does music fare? For no musical notation had as yet been developed, no fixed works of musical art, nor any theory taught in tracts, nor theoretically based tonal system, if only in its first rudiments. Is it justified then to call the Sumerian and Egyptian cultures "musical high cultures" without unduly extending the meaning of the term, or should one only speak of "the music *in* those high cultures"?

This music was in fact not in the same measure "high culture" as the music of classical Antiquity or of the West since the Middle Ages; the question is, *in how far* it nevertheless was a high culture. Its special nature has heretofore not been sufficiently examined. Classified under the general notion of "foreign cultures," it has been too little distinguished from the music of primitive and of later oriental peoples, while the great differences between it and the music of classical and later Antiquity have not been sufficiently emphasized. It behooves us in future, therefore, to take account of its original and basic achievements, upon which later times drew, as also to work out the differences between it and the music of those later times. Like every other epoch, this first period of our Second Age stood under "the immediacy of God." Our task is to grasp and coordinate its specific characteristics.

Erich Rothacker has stressed the point that the basic feature of high civilizations was the shaping of life on a "high" level, and that in this process art played an essential role. In Sumerian and Egyptian documents concerned with the music of their day this basic feature is evident. The dignified deportment of court musicians, the elegance and grace of the women, the discipline, intellectual and spiritual, of music-making groups—these are indicative of high stylization. Musical education in archaic high civilizations contributed to civility, nobility, and ethos.

It appears likewise that music participated in the elevated culture of city and court with new forms of its own. In its field too the new organization of society into lower, middle, and higher levels is seen. Painters, sculptors, and writers naturally do not tell of all these equally but primarily of cult and court, in which they served. The hierarchy is nevertheless evident, ranging from the singing country folk to audiences and connoisseurs at court, from mendicant musicians to court conductors. Not until society became thus organized were certain groups in the population, like the professional musicians, freed of the necessity to cooperate in material production. They were now wholly occupied in the service of art, cult, culture. Court orchestras and choirs came into being, types of the professional singer and instrumental virtuoso (like the distinguished, well-nourished, well-curled Assyrian performers in our illustration 4a), harems of girl musicians, and all else appertaining to musical life at court.

Beautifully decorated harps and other costly instruments bear witness to the magnificence of those days. The splendor of the god, the king, the court was to be audible as well as visible when trumpets and timbrels, lyres and harps, resounded. In the representation of power and glory music performed one of its chief functions in feudal societies. When the court musicians accompanied their sovereign at public appearances they gave sonorous expression to his majesty. Court and cult music combined to attest the sacred dignity of the king in his near-divinity. When he presented viands and libations to the gods, singers and instrumentalists participated in the formality. Thus in a Hittite ritual where the king and queen offer the various gods their beverage from the lion tankard and also one or more loaves of bread, between these two acts the text says each time: "The singer from the city of Kanesh sings."

The first high civilizations lay like islands in an ambience that still remained deep in the world's First Age. In the scope of its vitality Egyptian art did not fail to include representations of neighboring primitive peoples; for instance, of the dancing dwarves of Ethiopia. In Egyptian folk music too the First Age lived on, as well as in religious beliefs, customs, and the recreations and diversions of the upper classes. Eventually, with the stagnation of the higher style of life and the growing importance of the masses, retrogression set in, as we see, for example, in the renewed spread and significance of the animal cult in late Egyptian times.

Beside music for royal religious services and for court entertainment, sung incantation formulas were preserved and magic music to heal the sick. Numerous legends and fairy tales seem to have been told of the power of sounding tones; for example, that they had built city walls or caused them to fall down. Far and wide the gods were now being given human form, but in their animal heads and among the lower divinities and demons, like the lute-playing satyresque Bes of Egypt, oldtime myths survived and mask-games of half-human creatures. Many examples of animals as musicians are given by Emma Brunner-Traut,[2] who says there are countless such pictures known, but only a few

[2] In her books, *Die altägyptischen Scherbenbilder* (*Potsherd Paintings of Ancient Egypt*, 1956) and *Altägyptische Tiergeschichten* (*Ancient Egyptian Animal Stories and Fables, Saeculum*, 1959).

have as yet been published. They show, for example, a jackal playing for other animals to dance, a flute-playing fox, a dancing monkey playing oboe. In one a monkey leads his master, making him dance and playing the flute for him. Egyptian and Mesopotamian pictures often show whole orchestras of animals; a donkey harper, a crocodile lutenist, a meercat playing the double oboe, a lion playing a lyre to the singing of another lion. These pictures are variously interpreted, but they are certainly based on old familiar stories, many of which were also acted out; and in these animal musicians of ancient high cultures motifs from rites and mask-dramas must have survived. But what once was central to cult and belief has now become burlesque entertainment or passed into other secondary areas of life.

Music was interwoven with cult, court ceremonial, banquet and other supramusical activities. In these ancient high civilizations man was generally supposed, according to Freyer, "to implant his works in a natural landscape, elevating it to the realm of spirit." In these over-all sublimations music took a constructive and a consecrating part: in the building of temples and their permeation with the glory of their god, in processions along fields and rivers, in veneration of the sun and other acts celebrating the fecundity of nature. As formerly in hunting and agricultural rites, it now participated when animals and plants were sacrificed to the divinity. In a Cretan scene an aulos-player stands behind a sacrificial bull, and similar pictures have come down from all those ancient cultures.

The principal difference from prehistoric and early times lies for one thing in the fact that the supramusical contexts in which music now took part were in larger measure man-made and hence more independent of their natural surroundings: the temple has taken the place of the cave. In addition, music now entered into the activities more freely and for its own sake, as when towards the end of a feast singing and instrumental music were offered and enjoyed as fine entertainment. Further, music grew more independent with the independence of the musical profession. More notably, however, music took an important step from having been a secondary element to setting up a cultural field of its own in the making and maintenance of specific musical instruments that no longer served a variety of uses. The harp is not only more richly developed than the bow from which it sprang, but it serves music only, whereas the bow was simultaneously a weapon. It is a great achievement of the first high cultures that they created most of the musical instruments of Antiquity.

Besides these there were still many noise-making implements in use, sistra and other rattles, clappers, castanets. They were employed on their own account and also as accompaniment to vocal and instrumental melody. A dominant characteristic in the archaic production of sonorities is this setting of monophonic music as figuration, form, or design against a background of noise, shapeless and material, that shrouds the clarity of the musical tone. Like the drum, these implements evidently served not only to make "heathenish noises" but for disciplined and cultivated playing—to judge, for example, from the Egyptian custom of instructing several sistrum-players simultaneously. The same holds true of hand-clapping, everywhere used as accompaniment to dancing and music, which served, as pictures and surviving tradition show, not only to mark time but also for its sound-value, since it was performed alternatively with flat or cupped hands, and, like drum-playing, also rhythmically differentiated; why else should it have been taught?

The music of this period was nevertheless more closely linked with the body than that of later times. A singer often laid a hand to his temple, ear, cheek, or throat in order to modify the timbre of his voice, whether subjectively for himself or objectively for the listeners, as for instance by supporting the vibration of his vocal cords. More frequently than later, music, that dance of the soul, was still performed together with bodily dance; it was a part of the combined arts of the Muses. In how many pictures instrumentalists are shown striding or dancing! In processions, pageants, ritual scenes, one of their chief functions was to march or leap along with the participants. Dancing with an instrument, as one still finds it here and there in Turkey and elsewhere performed with a drum, was then in full flower. Playing in a seated or squatting position, and not only on stationary but also on portable instruments, was customary particularly in Egypt. To this corresponded the local chironomy, carried out no longer by instinctive gestures of hand and arm, but by means of specific signs.

Dancing with an instrument presupposes playing by heart. Dependence on the body goes with lack of a written score; emancipation from the body goes with a fixed musical notation. Before the Greeks, archaic high civilizations had developed no musical notation, or none at least that is traceable or likely to have been widespread; in this respect they were scriptless cultures. It is possible that the Phoenicians, who around 1500 B.C. accomplished the important change from syllabic to alphabetic writing, may also have invented the notation for the aulos that has been assumed, hypothetically, to be at the root of Greek instrumental notation; but so far no direct proof of this has been found. Efforts to prove the existence of a Babylonian musical notation have not been convincing; if here or there some writing down of tones occurred, it would have been only sporadic. The same holds true for music theory, first developed by the Greeks, even though oral transmission of technical precepts may already have contained some embryonic theory. It is a preconception to assume that the tuning of Sumerian and Egyptian instruments was based on a proper theory, indeed one mathematical and cosmological in character.

Music in these times had not yet been written down and to that extent freed from the actual playing; its tones had not yet been objectified in notes. Yet in the new sound-producing objects, in instruments like harp and lyre, it took on a more objective spirit than in prehistoric and early times when it had been for the most part no more than an element inherent in human action and one purpose of multipurposed utensils. A step towards objectification of tones was furthermore their transposition into clearly visible signs conveyed by hand and arm: chironomy. It is further quite likely that in ancient Mesopotamia especially, syllables came into use as names for tones. This is indicated by the fact, among others, that the series of scale-tone names, or solmizations, used in China, Bali, India, and medieval Europe have certain features in common which may best be explained by a common origin.

Quite probably the Carolingian solmization hymn to John the Baptist with its acrostic on the six syllables *ut re me fa sol la*—begging the saint to purify his servants' lips of sin that they may worthily sing his praises—may have its roots in an ancient tradition. In view of certain facts in old Mesopotamian culture it would not be surprising if such a root or proto-type were found there: one would think notably of the type of syllabic Babylonian acrostic that spread abroad after 1000 B.C., as well as of Ea or Oannes, revered as god of waters and of organizing forces, and invoked also as god who conjures purification and healing of the sick. But I would emphasize that this is only a surmise on my part and calls for further investigation.

E. M. von Hornbostel and other musicologists have assumed that astro-cosmological speculations known from later antique and oriental sources stem from archaic times and even then set the rules. Hornbostel thinks that the foundations of all musical life in Antiquity, which "were longest and most faithfully preserved in the Far East," probably go back "to a single source in the west-central Asia of the 4th or 5th millennium B.C." and that the Greeks had thence received, together with their instruments, "the string and pipe lengths determined by sanctified norms of measure" and "the absolute pitch and ordering of intervals thus laid down." According to this theory a common basis of "the musical culture of ancient times" would be "the construction of tonal systems and of instruments on extra-musical and ultimately cosmological principles, not the esthetic but the cultic and magic use of music."

The significance of number and measure in the division of time (12 months, 4 weeks, 7 days, 12 hours) and in other achievements of Mesopotamian civilization might speak in favor of these assumptions. Some pictures from this and other countries show musical ensembles consisting of seven persons (as in illus. 5a). Yet so many objections arise to challenge the theory that it may prove valid in only a very limited scope. In the first place, deductions drawn from Chinese testimony of a much later date about musico-cosmological views in early high cultures are extremely uncertain, and the oldest sources for musical theory and terminology in

China and India are not based on mathematics and cosmology but on practical classification. Similarly, it would be anachronistic to refer back to the beginnings of high cultures speculations that rest on Chaldean astrology—which hardly began before the 8th century B.C.—and its mixture with pagan gnosis.

Secondly, from what documentation we have of these cultures we cannot conclude that canonic numbers and extra-musical measure were widespread or even general norms for the practice of music. Thus in ancient oriental stringed instruments we know, according to Max Wegner, "neither 7 nor any other digit to rule the number of strings; instead we encounter an irregular variety of almost all numbers from 3 to 22, with 4, 5, and 8 occurring most frequently. . . . In the ancient Orient we can speak neither of any general norm nor of a defined number of strings for any particular type of instrument."

Thirdly, the Assyrians and others held the number 7 to be not only beneficent but also harmful and dangerous.

Fourthly, the frequent occurrence of the figures 5 and 7 in music does not necessarily rest on extra-musical norms, such as number symbolism, but like today's universal use of pentatonic and heptatonic systems, may be explained primarily on purely musical and psychological grounds; on the same grounds rhythms in $\frac{5}{4}$ and $\frac{7}{4}$ are less usual than scales of 5 and 7 steps.

Fifthly, the physiognomy and bearing of the musicians of those days—the Assyrian virtuosos and the Egyptian girl players, for example—contradict the assumption that they were not making beautiful music for polite society but giving themselves over to magic and cosmology.

And lastly one must consider that the real accomplishments of these peoples were based on real knowledge: speculation would not have enabled them to build monumental constructions like the Pyramids, nor to perfect the system of Babylonian mathematics (which anticipated the Pythagorean and solved equations with three and more unknown quantities). How significant it is that the first writing, that of Sumer and Egypt, served primarily a cold and realistic administration! Why should this spirit of the concrete and the real have been missing from their music and only immaterial speculation have ruled in its place?

The unrestricted assumption that magic and cosmological speculation governed the primitive conception of music is no longer tenable, just as Lévy-Bruhl's theory of a primitive mental process fundamentally different from logical thinking no longer holds. It must be replaced by historical research into the question of when, where, and how far magic, cosmology, and other speculations were really widespread and able to make their way against other factors, particularly against pragmatic craftsmanship and the practical understanding of the musician.

What we do know so far concerning the structure of music and singing in the early high civilizations does not deviate from the "natural orders" of *Gestalt* psychology that have held sway from prehistory to the present. That along-side irregular rhythms periodic beats too were widespread is apparent from the many documents that show walking and dancing in time to music. The wide use of percussion instruments and of handclapping must have favored such rhythm; so too would the organization of work and of military discipline in the newly developed state of society. Karl Bücher's ideas, in his *Arbeit und Rhythmus* (*Work and Rhythm*), apply far less to prehistoric and primitive times than to the communal and slave labor that was first fully developed in this Second Age.

Falkenstein and von Soden have pointed out that the Sumerians called the reciting of an incantation a "counting" of the text, and that this indicated a metrical structure. In Accadian, ancient Phoenician, and Hebrew verse only the number of strongly stressed arses was important, that of theses between them optional. "For most poetry of ancient times (before 1000 B.C.) the normal verse may be considered to have consisted of two half-verses with two stresses each, or a line with four accents, though this was not the only type used. Between those of four stresses other verses with three and five were inserted, mostly at irregular intervals." This combination of predominantly four-accent verses in free variety and freely filled with unstressed dips recalls a natural and widely used rhythm familiar to us from Old-European songs.

As in all times, earlier and later, the outstanding consonances were the octave, fifth, and fourth and these provided the framework. This is already evident in Egyptian chironomic signs and from the chords implied by the instruments and finger-stoppings indicated in pictures. According to Plutarch's commentary on the *Timeus* of Plato, the Chaldeans expressed the differences in the seasons by the fourth, the fifth, and the octave. A string on the long-necked lute could obviously be shortened at will by stopping at the half, the third, and so forth, to obtain the octave, the fifth, etc. Lyre and harp players may, as Curt Sachs explains, have relied on their ear, "and the ear applies three innate standards at once: the intervals of the octave, the fifth, and the fourth." Starting from a median tone, for example c, they probably tuned the fifth above (g), then the fourth below that (d) and the fifth again above this (a), and so forth. Dissimilar to a theoretical principle like the Pythagorean cycle of fifths, this up-and-down system of fifths and fourths is a handy practical principle for tuning instruments with several strings. That it first yields a pentatonic system without semitones (c, d, e, g, a) is obvious.

While the simplest pitch relationships, i.e. consonances, are thus obtainable on stringed instruments, the boring of fingerholes in wind instruments on a similar pattern would give complex irrational intervals. In the high cultures as in the primitive these holes were not spaced so as to give the intervals customary on stringed instruments or in singing, but simply at equal distances from each other. Such equidistance, not of tones but of fingerholes, automatically excludes any musical scale; but this could be approximated by other means. The pitch was modified by the breath of the player, by different sizes of hole and further, by covering the hole completely or partially with the finger. In addition, a general law of musical psychology permits the ear to tolerate slight divergencies and accept them as correct. In playing with voices and strings the wind-instrumentalist would have adjusted his intervals to theirs.

It is very probable, on the other hand, that the oboe and similar instruments gave rise to the "chromatic" coloration of pitches and, as a consequence, to the use of halftones and microtones. Heinrich Husmann suggests that the enharmony of the Greeks stems from Syria. Presumably it was here that those modified and "peculiar" intonations of pitch began that today are considered typically oriental: they would seem to have been transmitted from wind instruments to singing and to stringed instruments.

GREEK AND ROMAN ANTIQUITY

The Second Age of Music may be divided into three periods, the first of which embraces the early high cultures. The second period opens with the beginning of musical theory and concepts of philosophy of music, first developed in Greece and China at a time that stood under the influence of approximately contemporary prophets and founders of great religions, who had come to the fore particularly in India, Persia, and Israel. The third period includes the survival of Antiquity in the Orient and the further course of music in the high cultures of that part of the world.

From the standpoint of universal history, Greco-Roman Antiquity seems to have been far less important in the realm of music than in those of philosophy, poetry, sculpture, and architecture. Only a few fragments have been preserved in musical notation, and their effect is scant and colorless; they offer only monophonic lines with no indication of accompaniment, coloring, or character. Almost all of them stem from late Antiquity and none is an impressive composition. It is true that great poets, like Alkaios, Sappho, Pindar, Aeschylus, Euripides, Horace, were also creative musicians, but this part of their activities lies shrouded in mystery.

The level of a culture, however, is not established only on the work it leaves behind, but also on the realities it has lived through and the influences it has called into being. In both respects Greco-Roman Antiquity is of great significance in the history of music too. How important the art of music was in Greek culture is evident from the high favor it enjoyed in comparison to the other arts. The art of fashioning human beings rated higher with the Greeks than the art of shaping stones. To be "musikos," that is, to make oneself a cultured person, was considered worthier than devotion to the plastic arts. It also accorded with their ordering of society and the splendor of their newly developed theories that intellectual and spiritual contemplation should be more highly esteemed than working with one's hands, which set the sculptor and the mere instrumentalist on a level with the craftsman.

The Greeks left no treasure in musical works of art but they lived a great historical hour in musical culture. It was they also who first laid the foundations of scholarship in music, its terminology and notation, its theory and philosophy. Broad currents of tradition flowed from their music and their music theory through Rome, Byzantium, and the Arabian empire, to the Near East and onwards to the Far East. Fundamental Greek terms—tone, rhythm, melos, harmony—are today universally valid and all mankind calls the tonal art by the Greek name of "music." Furthermore, the music of Greek Antiquity, although—and perhaps also because—it did not reveal itself in any great compositions, became during the Renaissance a fruitful stimulus for the rise of opera and other creations of Western music.

The Religious and Ethical Meaning of Music

The word "music" has its origin in Greek religion: music is the only art named after a divinity. Mythology speaks as well of several muses as of a single divinity, the Muse; Homer, Hesiod, and other poets invoke the Muse at the opening of their works to aid memory and inspiration. In essence and in action the Muse seems to have been related to creative Nature, who controls the growth of living things. Various radiations from this force, representing various of its attributes, become the Muses, who, led by the god Apollo, dance their rounds on lonely mountain meadows, akin to the nymphs as the poem is to the flower.

Singers and players of the kithara descend like sons from Apollo and the Muses, says Hesiod. Odysseus tells Demodocus he respects him above all men because the Muse, daughter of Zeus, or Apollo himself has taught him. The gods, from whom music comes and whom music celebrates, are considered the *eidos*, the ideal image, of man, but man at the same time is made in the image of the gods; they are anthropomorphic, man theomorphic. The noble singer to the kithara is modeled after Apollo, and Apollo is represented as an idealized kitharode; the figure of the god and the *eidos* of the musician merge. Apollo the archer and at the same time player of the lyre or the kithara, is the prototype of a being purely human in contrast to the satyr Marsyas, who might stand for the primitive bowman and sorcerer in an animal mask (see illus. 2a). He is the purely human god, contrasting also with goat-footed Pan and the satyrs, in whom the mythological animal-man of primitive times and the older high cultures has survived.

Orpheus too, who charms and tames wild animals by the power of music, carries along prehistoric myth and custom on the high level of musical art (cf. illus. 1 and 2a). The implication here concerns wildness, not only external to ourselves but also within us. This is clear from a picture on a mixing jug of around 450 B.C. The Thracean Orpheus here plays the lyre before four Thracian wariors armed with spears. One of them seems to turn, somber and unresponsive, from the music, but the others are charmed, spellbound. The Greeks, says Herder, "did not have the word humanity; but after Orpheus had made them from beasts into men by the sound of his lyre, the concept of this word became the art of their Muses." Like Orpheus, "all partners in Greek art, Linus, Musaeus, Eumolpus, Homer, and whoever worthily touched the strings . . . had their share in this immortal glory of having made men human. . . . Song the Greeks cultivated at festivals and at the joyous board, at altars, at public games and on the battlefield. Song followed them into the realm of the dead and there alleviated the terrors of Hades. Thus whatever of good in Greek culture fell to the share of other peoples they owed originally to the lyre." "The lyre of Orpheus has rightly been placed among the stars; it did more than Hercules's club; it made brutes human."

Mythology represented different kinds of music and their mutual relationships through portraying gods and demons and their rivalries. The musical contest between Apollo and the satyr Marsyas symbolizes the coming to terms of the great Apollonian undercurrent in advanced high culture with the wild natural heritage of prehistoric times; representatives of these two Ages of music here confront each other. But so long as the Greek spirit lived it did not posit the Apollonian idea as a classic absolute, but kept natural vitality as a counterbalance. Pan, Dionysus, and lower divinities inebriate with the procreative urge were not put aside in doctrinaire manner in favor of Apollo, but honored as powers belonging to the totality of the divine world and to human life which follows in its wake. "The Greeks too," says Herder, "were once . . . wild, and even in the flower of their finest period there is much more of Nature than the blinking eyes of the scholiasts and classicists can find. . . . And when Arion, Orpheus, Amphion lived they were but noble Greek shamans." Accordingly in the manifold unity of mythology old types of music maintained their place beside the new, the more vital beside the more spiritual. Alongside Apollo's lyre stand the shrill oboe-like species of the aulos (often quite falsely translated as flute) which particularly corresponds to the domain of Dionysus, and the syrinx called, after the god of free nature and of shepherds, panpipe.

In this undogmatic manner mythology taught how music can contribute to civilization. In his battle against the secularizing Sophists Plato sought to preserve this ethical significance and to renew it: this art of the Muses was given us "so that men, nourishing themselves in solemn intercourse with the gods, may receive direction and rectitude anew." The founding of philosophy in the full sense of the word led to the renewal also of the ethical meaning of music. Plato gave a fresh impetus to ideas that underlay religious tradition and fixed them in philosophical concepts. At the same time, however, he rejected whatever he thought deleterious to the idea of man and the moral underpinnings of society. He wished to banish from his ideal state the music of Dionysus and his aulos. He was thus strictly perpetuating a mythological theme represented, for example, in a 5th-century sculpture, according to which it was Athena who invented the aulos, but she cast it away and struck the satyr Marsyas when he took it to himself.

Thus in Greek notions about the ethos of music mythical and philosophical motifs intermingle, as do efforts at attaining broader scope with the limitations set by stricter purification. Around this kernel speculation swarmed, and superstition. Again and again the same singular fables were repeated; they were the commonplaces transmitted from Antiquity into the Middle Ages and beyond. When at the close of Antiquity Boethius wishes to prove the ethical influence of music, he does not offer verifiable facts of his own time but calls to mind an ancient fable: "For who would not know that Pythagoras brought to his senses a drunken youth driven mad by a Phrygian tune, by singing him a spondaic melody?"

Partisans of Greek enlightenment and sobriety, on the other hand, unmasked the ethos doctrine. An Athenian orator of Plato's day, for example, finds fault with people who pursue vague speculations about music and ethos but fail as practical musicians. If they claim that enharmony engenders manly courage, why, then, are singers of the theater, who excel in enharmonic melody, much less courageous than their neighbors of Thermopylae, who can only sing diatonically?

But more important than either the sentimental enthusiasm or the mockery that surrounded the teaching of ethos is the intelligible core of the doctrine itself. That through the ear music penetrates the inner self and contributes to the forming of character, insofar as musical education is confined to impressing on the individual certain styles in relation to certain types of behavior, is not an irresponsible notion but a perfectly valid fact. Those who reflected upon the question knew that the ethos of a given music is not something palpable and permanent, like a hard stone, but like an idea, to be worked on: Dorian music is not "manly" in itself, but conveys a stimulus to the *aretē* or ethical virtue of virility. Only a person by nature disposed to this *aretē* can meet the challenge and realize it. Dorian melodies, it was said, could not make a hero of the cowardly Thersites, but an Achilles they could nourish and strengthen.

Two other essential features of Greek musical culture are linked with the basic concept of ethos: *agon*, competition, and *paideia*, education. In rivalry, and particularly in the great national contests, the musician developed and intensified his skill; measuring his accomplishments against those of others and endeavoring to surpass them, he rose above himself. And during his instruction the pupil not only was trained *in* music, he was trained *by* it. An Attic bowl of 485–80 B.C. shows teacher and pupil playing the lyre (illus. 7b) as well as lessons in aulos-playing, writing, and recitation. The art of music, Plato says, is the most important part of education, because rhythm and harmonious successions of tones penetrate deepest into the soul and tend to good form and good bearing. Anyone correctly brought up will also have a keen sense of the inadequate in art and in Nature. From this he will keep his distance; but beautiful forms and images he will take with joy into his soul, fashion himself after them and thus become *kaloskagathos*, "noble in character and conduct."

Science and the Mystique of Numbers; Theory and Notation

Musicology has been called the youngest of the sciences of art, but it is in truth the oldest. In the form of music history, to be sure, it did not develop until later, and not fully until the 18th century; but in the form of basic canons of musical doctrine it had already in Antiquity become a branch of knowledge, a learned discipline. From the 4th century B.C. and for the first time in the evolution of music, we have texts that deal specifically with its theory.

The mathematical foundation of this knowledge was established by the later Pythagoreans; its roots lie in the early Pythagorean mystique of numbers. As a theory—that is, as reflection upon natural laws—it made use of numbers, for numbers were what was real and dependable in the world, they were held to be cosmic principles: they could be laid out on the canonic monochord as numerical relations—1 : 2 : 3 : 4—and could be heard in the corresponding intervals. Pythagoras himself drew on Mesopotamian and Egyptian sources.[1] He did not, however, merely take over confused oriental traditions and illumine them with the light of Greek reason; a man rich in knowledge, he was also a dark dreamer who was honored as a prophet and worker of miracles. Heraclitus reproached him with having no rational insight, only particularized knowledge, and being, with his private system, the "captain of the charlatans." The religious fraternity he founded sought to achieve purity of soul through ascetic monasticism and through music; by means of initiation into the mysteries of eternal numbers and of cosmic harmony they strove to escape the cycle of reincarnation. In music the Pythagoreans thought to recognize that everything in the world is ordered by numbers, especially by the *tetrakis* 1, 2, 3, 4. To this last they attribute the most various instances: "What is the oracle of Delphi? The *tetrakis!* For that is the musical scale of the Sirens." Number, harmony, and music seemed to raise the soul to divinity in their teaching. "Mathematics and the mystique of numbers," says van der Waerden, "were mixed in fantastic fashion. But from this mystic doctrine the exact science of the later Pythagoreans evolved." Soon after Pythagoras's death his disciples parted. Those who followed the more scientific direction with Hippasus, Archytas, and others developed the four *mathemata*, the four disciplines that later were looked upon as essential to erudition (*enkyklios paideia*) and that passed over into the four *artes liberales* of the Middle Ages: arithmetic, music, geometry, astronomy. But the speculative tendency of the mystique of numbers also continued; revived by the Neo-Pythagoreans in late Antiquity, it too carried over into the Middle Ages.

[1] As is shown by, among others, B. L. van der Waerden in his *Erwachende Wissenschaft,* 1956.

A second type of music theory was laid down by Aristoxenus in terms of the philosophical science of Aristotle. He trusted the ear more than the Pythagoreans and Plato did, and instead of investigating only the mathematical basis of music measurable on the monochord, he spotlighted the audible phenomena themselves. Thoughtfully, expertly, and clearly he built upon controllable experiment and precise concepts with Aristotelian logic and systematics. He started from the smallest units of measure: in pitch with the whole tone, in rhythm with a value of short duration (the *chronos protos*), and with methodical abstraction distinguished between, for example, the rhythm itself and the rhythmic sequence of tones, words, steps.

Among later authors Ptolemy and Aristides Quintilian stand out; all of them limited musical science to consideration of the world of tone (intervals and scales, melody, rhythm) and certain sections of philosophy and ethics. It would be one-sided to see the achievement of Greek and Roman music theory before Boethius as merely the dogmatization of a practice, whether this practice is considered to be the musical language of Antiquity as a whole, the grammar of which was written by the Greeks, or "early 5th-century music" canonized by them in terms of a conservative classical ideology. More important than the dogmatics of a limited time-period are the real knowledge and the fundamental concepts that form the heart of it. This solid matter has become the basis of systematic musicology and has merged into it as the kernel of antique logic and mathematics has merged into the general advance of science.

In myth, philosophy, and theory it was the Greeks who first put into words the primary phenomena of music. They fixed these in basic concepts, for example that of "harmonia," which Heraclitus perceptively called the concord of opposites. The Greeks of course did not create these phenomena, but they moved them into another sphere, an intellectual sphere. Rhythm, melody, harmony were a heritage from earlier cultures and had already been realized in various forms when the Greeks entered upon the scene of history. But they raised them more explicitly to an intellectual level, into ideal objects of contemplative thought. They considerably reinforced the share of objectivity of mind—a heightened objectivity—in the total complex of musical culture.

The rise of notation led in the same direction. If writing is a way for man to attain spiritual domination over his world, the writing of music plays its part in this. Its contribution consists in the setting down of music in visible signs, on stone or papyrus, fixing it in enduring forms. It objectivizes the sounds, abstracts them from the concrete action, and perpetuates them as idea objectified.

Through his studies of vase paintings Egert Pöhlmann has demonstrated that musicians played from written notes as early as the 5th century B.C. (cf. illus. 5b); which indicates that creative musicians already at that time wrote down melodies. In the 2nd century B.C. rhythmography and melography are mentioned now and then as subjects in student examinations. The number of pieces so far found is nevertheless very small (some 33), though a few have been added in recent years. This is partly because the older theorists, even Aristoxenus, held notation in contempt, considering it ignoble, for which reason also it was not collected in libraries. Quite otherwise than in the Middle Ages, theory and notation were separated from one another; theoretical writings contain no musical examples. Thus not only have few pieces of music been preserved in writing, but only few were written down. Even in Antiquity the classics of sung poetry were generally known only from verbal texts. Thus the Greeks, while they took the historically important step to the notation of music, did not transform musical culture into a script culture to anything like the extent that the Middle Ages did. They clung for the most part to the practice that by and large distinguishes our First and Second Ages from the Third and Fourth: they created, preserved, and transmitted music without writing it down.

Melody and Polyphony

The Greek melodies that have come down to us are in the main cast in simple and, in terms of *Gestalt* psychology, "natural" orders. The tune of the Seikilos Song, an epigrammatic skolion in an epitaph of the 1st century A.D. (cf. music ex. 23c), is the model of a singable melody. It is clearly divided into four groups of two measures, corresponding to the four lines of the epigram. The rhythm, indicated not only by the meter of the text but also by the usual marks for short and long notes, is a regular $\frac{6}{8}$. The melody is purely diatonic, stressing the consonances in two triadic sequences, one leap of a fifth, the octave interval between the first quarter note and the last, and generally in the disposition of the notes. This eight-measure melody represents the basic model of the plastic and symmetrical strophic song which is familiar to us from the folksongs of Europe, and which had already been widespread in early rural and pastoral cultures of northern Asia, Europe, and America. Very likely the Greeks and Romans cultivated plastic forms of melody especially. Many of the strophic songs of which only the texts have been preserved may have been sung to melodies similar in construction to the Seikilos fragment. This would correspond with that predominance of pregnant natural structures in the sculpture and architecture of Antiquity which we call classic.

Other sources also show a notable proportion of triadic phrases and even of major melody. A 2nd-century monophonic fragment, published in 1959 by Turner and Winnington-Ingram, contains the phrases g-e-c-g-g and, in $\frac{6}{8}$, e′/ē′-g′-d̄′-c′/c̄′-b-c′-d′-c′/a-a-g. An instrumental piece begins with c-f-a-c′-b♭-a-g-f (transposed) and closes with f-c-c′-a. This reminds one of ancient Chinese zither melodies (e.g. f-c′-c-c′-a-g-f-c′-c-c′, etc.) and also of the earliest examples of the instrumental music of medieval minstrels. Melody thus rich in consonances (partly in half-tone-less pentatonic, partly in major or major-like tonalities) was probably widespread even among the nations of Antiquity, and it may well be that European round-dance melodies and minstrel music stem from this widely distributed style rather than from certain specific traditions.

Consonances also provided the framework of the tonal system. The importance of the tetrachord concept indicates the primacy of the fourth, the standard also for the strings ("four-stringed"), and establishes the interval of the second; as with the medieval hexachords a chief problem in teaching and practice was to inculcate musically exact seconds instead of depending on the approximations of the voice, and in so doing to distinguish whole tone, half tone, and microtones. The chromatic system was distinguished from the diatonic by its consecutive semitones (music ex. 24a), the enharmonic by its quarter tones. Yet these last belonged, as in the later Near East and India, rather to the tonal system than to melody; they were the smallest theoretical units, but it is unlikely that several quarter tones were actually played consecutively. Besides, enharmonic music did not last long and was not generally diffused in the society. According to Aristides Quintilian diatonic melody was considered natural (*genos physikotēron*) and singable even by the uninitiate, while chromatic melody should only be performed by those schooled in the art, and enharmonic only by a small elite.

That rhythm did not come from the measure as scheme of time-division does not mean that measured rhythm in the broader sense of the word was lacking in the performance of music in those days. The regular beat in dance and march obviously provided a natural rhythmic basis. This is apparent from the concepts of verse-foot, arsis and thesis, which correspond with periodic movements of the body. A vase painting shows the marching in step of soldiers led by aulos-players,[2] and Thucydides reports that in contrast to the Argives and others who rush in violent disorder to the attack, the Lacedaemonians incorporated numerous aulos-players in their ranks "for the sake of making a regular, rhythmic advance."

Varied use was made of asymmetrical rhythms, like $\frac{5}{8}$, $\frac{7}{8}$, $\frac{10}{8}$, etc., or more exactly: $1\frac{1}{2}$ quarters $+$ 1 quarter ($\frac{5}{8}$), or 1 quarter $+$ 1 quarter $+$ $1\frac{1}{2}$ quarters ($\frac{7}{8}$). Aristoxenus called these *podes alogoi*, irrational feet, and systematized them. In the Balkans and in the Orient they have been preserved as *aksak*, so-called Bulgarian rhythm, or developed in other forms. In the Antique world, they were probably widely diffused, far beyond Greece.

The biased view that the music of Antiquity was monophonic

[2] Friedrich Behn, *Musikleben im Altertum*, 1954, Plate 59, no. 137.

on principle is as little valid as that which would set contrapuntal polyphony back into the Second Age. That elementary forms of polyphony, like the interspersion of single chords for accentuation, or an accompanying bourdon (especially on instruments with two pipes), or simultaneous variants, or free unison, may have been customary appears both from an inherent likelihood and from traditions of the Mediterranean area. A higher form of polyphony was the "heterophonia" to which Plato attests in the *Laws*, where he recommends avoiding it if one has studied music for only three years; from his description, the accompanying lyre diverged from the vocal line through wider intervals, denser sequences of tones, different rhythms. The occurrence of chords is also confirmed elsewhere in literary documentation. The paradoxical formulas for harmony beloved in the Middle Ages, like *dissonantia concors*, go back to Antiquity. Phrases like *synadon diadon* (Heraclitus), *concentus dissonus* (Seneca), *symphonia discors* (Horace) stand sometimes for a confusion of voices, as during a meal or a concert of birds, sometimes for musical chords.

Abundant testimony shows that in Antiquity a multicolored fulness of sounds was cultivated by the playing together of many instruments, supported and enveloped by noise-making implements. Intensity of sound was also achieved by means of sounding-boards and resonators. It is a prejudice of classicists to represent the music of Antiquity as always linear and always gentle.

Evolution and Change

Original and fundamental as was the achievement of the Greeks in music, it is true that this comparatively late civilization took over a great deal, partly at the start, partly in the course of its history, from primitive and early times, from older high cultures and from neighboring countries. The Greeks bear witness to this themselves in that they named their modes after oriental regions (Lydian or Phrygian, for example) and assumed that certain of their mythical singers and musicians, like Orpheus, Olympus, Thaletas, were of Thracian, Phrygian, Cretan origin.

The history of Greek poetry from the pre-Homeric *aoidē* to Hellenistic times has a musical side of considerable importance, much of which might be better clarified than heretofore by means of more refined methods. Most of its verse and strophic forms, including the hexameter, were originally song forms; to interpret them from a purely philological angle does not do justice to this fact. That Alcaeus composed his lyric poems to the lyre, or Alcman his songs to the aulos, might mean among other things that Greek poets adhered to definite rhythmic and musical models customarily employed in the style used for each of these instruments, to the extent at least that they did not themselves introduce new tonal patterns, new "modes."

The contrast between lyre and aulos cannot have been as great in practice as in the later ethos doctrine, for these two instruments were often used together, as both literary and pictorial sources indicate. Singing to the aulos and aulos-playing by itself were on the whole the more free, more varied, more dynamic in capacity for change. Here it was that enharmony developed and its corresponding notation, and furthermore types of characteristically musical rhythm and the sort of mimesis that is called tone-painting and program music. Countries surrounding the Mediterranean preserved among other traditions from Antiquity the genre of musical story-telling to a single wind instrument. Robert Lachmann has found among the Bedouin a remarkable parallel to the special type of Pythian nomos that Sakadas of Argos performed at the Delphic games in 586 B.C. In the one, Apollo's fight with the dragon, in the other a Bedouin's battle with a lion, is related in program music on a single wind instrument, and both in five movements; in the latter as in the former (we have a detailed description of the Pythian nomos) a kind of fanfare-like melodic figure was used for picturing the battle, and overblowing employed as one technical way of achieving color.

The change in the plastic arts that set in around 430 B.C., after the flowering of the "grand style," and brought in a period of transition that lasted till the beginning of Hellenism around 320, reminds one of what happened in music around 1600. To judge from polemical and other sources the new music around Phrynis and Timotheus was multicolored and multiform; Pherecrates compared Phrynis to the whirlwind, which turns things upside down, and reproached him for his exuberant and motley style. Aristophanes made fun of the "ants' pricklings" of the virtuosos and flourishes sung to oft-repeated syllables. The art of music grew more independent in its relation to poetry and dance, and instrumental music came more strongly to the fore. In painting, withdrawal into and absorption in the private world of music were now frequently depicted. Euripides and others sought to link "monody," solo song, closely with verbal accent and give it passionate expression.

The secularizing influence of the Sophists created in connection with these artistic currents a historically important challenge to the forces of tradition. In his critique of the tendencies of his time, including those in music, Plato developed a conservative ideology, but above and beyond that, too, philosophic thoughts that transcended time, much as Jacob of Liège was to do around 1300 in his polemic against *ars nova*, or Hugo Riemann, at the beginning of our own century, in his efforts to rescue and safeguard the foundations of Western music.

Music in Hellenistic Times and in the Roman Empire

It would be a mistake to maintain that there is a correspondence in Oswald Spengler's sense between late Antiquity and the beginnings of our global industrial era, but it may help clarify our subject to call attention to a few similarities. In both Hellenistic times and the Roman Empire a culture became widely diffused and led to syncretism. Centers like Alexandria and Rome not only radiated their influence in every direction but at the same time took to themselves a great variety of Greek kitharists, Syrian dancers, oriental cult musicians, Negroes, and so forth.

Characteristic for the new music culture was the mass attraction it exercised in theater and circus, in music for entertainment, in its popular "hits." The wealthy had slaves at their disposal as we today have radio and records; the master had but to command whatever he wished, the music was played for him: "iubet citharam loqui—psallitur; tibias agere—sonatur; choros canere—cantatur" (he orders the kithara to speak—it is played; the flutes to sound—they sound; the chorus to sing—it sings).

Dion of Prosa in Bithynia gives a vivid picture of the cult of stardom in the 1st century A.D. The audience are beside themselves and hail the virtuoso as a savior and god. They leap from their seats in excitement, higher than dancers. Lucian sings the praises of pantomime, the grand ballet of those days, as the peak to which the arts of the Muses have climbed from the most primitive beginnings: the visible and the audible, the psychic and the physical, song and the playing of instruments—all these components, and in them the Muses themselves, worked together, so that there had arisen a perfect art of all the arts. People sang in the streets what they had heard in the theater. The young people know no psalms, John Chrysostomos complains, but every evening they go through the city singing obscenities (*pornika melē*) and impious songs (*satanika asmata*). When Galba became emperor, the entire public at a theatrical performance joined in the refrain of a popular hit (*notissimum canticum*) that made allusion to Galba's avarice; so Suetonius reports.

This massward drive engendered a tendency in the opposite direction. The higher classes of society and separatist or esoteric groups withdrew into an esthetic self-sufficiency or a nostalgic glorification of better times, others into an idyllic unreality, still others into religious sects or into metamusical speculation. Esthetic self-sufficiency is expressed in the saying that someone sings only for himself and the Muses (*sibi tantum caneret et musis*). Politically powerless and artistically unproductive, the Graeculi, the late Greeks, gave themselves over to ancient traditions, either through reflection upon them—as in the document attributed to Plutarch on the classic Greek music of yore—or through pious restoration—as when at the close of the 2nd century two Delphic hymn tunes were immortalized in inscriptions. The withdrawal into the rural idyll led to the imaginary landscape of Arcadia and the pastoral style: in his *Grammar* Diomedes says of bucolic poetry, which was also sung, that it was said to be composed on the model of shepherds' songs (*Bucolica dicuntur poemata secundum carmen pastorale composita*). Theoretic spirits saw in rational contemplation the only worthy approach to music. The science of it, says Boethius, stands as high above practical music-making as the mind above the body. In his commentary on Plato's *Timaeus*, Chalcedius, in the 4th century, places rational divine music (*musica divina*), the only true music, over against that which serves the enjoyment of the masses (*ea musica qua vulgus delectatur*). The Neo-Pythagoreans and others pursuing similar lines speculated upon an intelligible metamusic of which anything that was perceptible to the ear was but a shadow.

It would show a lack of critical acumen to assume that the view sustained by this particular tendency was that of late Antiquity in general. In comparison with the mass-directed activity of the time and with the other special groups, it could have counted only within a limited circle. According to Claudius Mamertus, music as a mathematical discipline was often held in as much abhorrence as the Furies. The music theory of late Antiquity, as well as a few other special tendencies, nevertheless unleashed effects of great importance historically. What was written down endured, what was widely practiced perished. Boethius in particular became for the Middle Ages and for humanism the chief representative of Antiquity, not because he was a high point in its musical life, but because his writings had been preserved among the very few documents concerning music and music theory.

It has become a commonplace to think that the music of Italy during the Roman Empire gave way in part to luxury and decadence, in part to moral sobriety and military forms. That this is a misconception Günther Wille has shown in an extensive dissertation backed by many proofs. Methodical research into Italian music of Antiquity and of the Empire has become a new theme in music history. Traces in popular traditions and in Latin liturgical song, together with the study of Latin poetry, offer the possibility of finding out something not only about the musical life of Roman Antiquity but also about the music itself.

JEWISH AND CHRISTIAN ANTIQUITY

The Trend towards Spirituality and Inwardness
Gregorian chant, upon which the Catholic Church has built the enduring basis of her liturgical music, juts like a great erratic boulder into the present. As a whole it was laid down in the Middle Ages, but its constituent elements and its melodic types go back in part to Christian Antiquity, and its roots are still older; they are to be sought in the Jewish religious service and further back in those earliest high cultures and high cults that in many forms of prayer and attitudes of the praying bring to mind the Catholic Middle Ages. The biblical psalms plainchant uses as texts and which have determined its designs and rhythms are related in form to the hymns of the Sumerians and the Phoenicians.

On the other hand, Gregorian chant differs radically from such archaic cult music in that it totally excludes instruments and ritual dance and is widely performed today without clearly defined, indeed without regularly pulsating, rhythm. These and other differences are the result of historical processes that in part took place during the Middle Ages (like the loss of ancient prose rhythm), in part were already at work in Jewish and Christian Antiquity. The evolution into the second period of Antiquity, in which philosophy and science were born, was simultaneously determined by new religious forces. While one aspect of this evolution took place particularly in Greece and China, leading to philosophy and ethics, to musical theory and notation, in the religious evolution Israel came to the fore, to which Christianity and, later, Islam were linked. Here, most decisively and with important consequences for the future, God had come to be considered a unique Being, immaterial and spiritual. He was now no longer represented in animal forms, in stones, in human shapes; he became a disembodied personality to be worshipped, prayed to, loved as a father. In strict opposition to "heathen" cults, the worship of a plurality of gods and of the image was herewith rejected, or at least, as in the wake of Christendom triumphant, severely modified. Liturgical singing too became more or less dematerialized and, as prayer to God as a person, interiorized, spiritualized. The destiny of the Jewish people, the destruction of the Temple, the Babylonian Captivity, and the later Diaspora fostered the aversion to cult music of varied timbre and color.

This was, of course, only the underlying characteristic of the evolution. Some of its strands proved but transient, others were lastingly woven in. As was to be the case in the Middle Ages and in modern times, various tendencies worked together or against each other in their efforts to achieve various types and degrees of spiritualization: from the linkage with pagan forms, through selection and sublimation of inherited elements, to radical asceticism. In the process various motifs from Hellenic and Hellenistic Antiquity were absorbed, drawn from traditions both sensuous and spiritual. Thus Philo of Alexandria (1st century) contrasts true music, ethical and cosmic, with the effeminate, sensual music in use at banquets and in the theater. Then again, opposing trends were brought into this synthesis, both by the Church in general and by individual thinkers, St. Augustine (4th century) in particular.

The basic trend to dematerialization affected all branches of music; for the spirit's sake everything that belonged to the physical part of singing and of tone was brought into question. Instruments, in the first place, had had until now their sacred aura and dignity, especially trumpets and other wind instruments, and belonged to the normal accompaniment of ritual singing, like the kinnor of the Hebrews, a box lyre. When at the consecration of the Temple hundreds sang and played together "and it was as though one alone trumpetted and sang . . . then did the glory of the Lord fill the House of God." The Synagogue, on the contrary, both the early and the late, confined itself to chant without instruments. After the restoration of the Second Temple this abstention was observed as a sign of national religious mourning, but other motives must also have contributed to the interdiction. Early Christendom too kept instruments out of divine service, and the Orthodox Church maintained this exclusion while the Western Church later took in the organ and other instruments. On the acceptance of instruments in the rest of Christian musical life opinions differed. Clement of Alexandria rejected syrinx and aulos as more suitable to animals than to men, and among the latter only to the less spiritual; but others he accepted: "If thou wouldst sing to the kithara or the lyre, thou shalt bear no blame, for thereby thou doest what the righteous king of the Jews did who was well-pleasing to God."

To the interiorization of the chant belonged further the exclusion of ritual dance, attested to of old in so many examples: not only the dance around a god in animal form, e.g. the golden calf, but also David's dance before the Ark of the Covenant, the dancing of Miriam's women with the song of triumph after the passage of the Red Sea, and others. With the elimination of ritual dance also took place the transformation of Hebraic poetry from rhythmically constructed verse to plain prose.

Further elements in this development were the limiting of music to strict unison, which became the Christian symbol of unanimity (*unanimitas*), as well as the almost total exclusion of women from liturgical chant. For the teaching of singing in the home St. Jerome recommended that no pretty singer with a glib voice be selected, but rather a serious spinster of advanced years, shabbily dressed and somewhat sad, who should teach the pupil how to sing the horary prayers "standing at attention like a female soldier of Christ": "Placeat ei comes non compta atque formosa, quae liquido gutture carmen dulce moduletur, sed gravis, pallens, sordidata, subtristis. Praeponatur ei . . . virgo veterana, quae illam doceat et assuescat exemplo ad orationes et psalmos nocte consurgere, mane hymnos canere, tertia, sexta, nona hora stare in acie quasi bellatricem Christi."

Finally the question arose, should there be singing at all?

Synagogue and Catholic Church, indeed, preserved the usual chant (in the Evangelical Church spoken word and congregational singing alternate) but the principle of singing inwardly (*intus canere*) or with the heart, not with the mouth (*corde, non ore*), was taken by many to mean entirely silent singing. Others believed that only intoning of the lessons and recitative-like psalmody accorded with Word and Spirit, whereas all singing with any melodic or musical value implied an absence of the strict religious sense. In a pedagogical dialogue of the 4th century a pupil of old Abbot Pambo complains that he had admired the church choirs in Alexandria, the great city, and is very sad that the monks in the desert do not also sing their canons and their tropes. At which the old man says to him: "Woe unto us, son, that the days have come when monks desert the firm, strong nourishment of the Holy Ghost and deliver themselves over to lyric singing and music . . . Surely the monks did not move out into the desert to step proudly before God performing melodies, singing in rhythmically various modes, clapping their hands and moving their feet in dance steps. No, we must in fear and trembling, with tears and sighs, pious and penitent, with discreet and humble voices recite our prayers to God." In his *Confessions* (X, 33) St. Augustine presents a similar contention, an argument not between two persons but with himself: he sometimes wishes that all beautiful melody were banished from the Church, but then he thinks how his soul is moved and shaken by it, and that the textual content, penetrating through the melody, works the more impressively.

Temple and Synagogue

That music is spoken of much more often in the Old Testament than in the New is significant. The references are supplemented by the rich traditions in archaic synagogal chants, among which those from Yemen, Persia, and Mesopotamia stand out because in the oldest of them a common heritage from the time before the Babylonian exile may well have been preserved. Gathered together in the Archives of Musical Recordings at Jerusalem, these documents offer fertile possibilities for a comparative study of melody. They are a prime source for ancient Jewish music and also for the musical roots and beginnings of Christendom (cf. music exx. 9 ff.).

These melodies clearly reveal an archaic prose rhythm distinct both from Gregorian tunes as performed today and from measured, equally pulsating rhythms. They consist of motif-formulas in which small running starts of a few notes, stopping points of held tones, and cadences together provide a rhythmic pattern. Shorter and longer notes alternate, though they are not so exactly proportioned as, say, the halves and quarters in $\frac{3}{4}$ time. A series of short notes is sung as upbeat approach to a longer note or a warbling motif is twice or thrice repeated, enhancing the musical intensity that presses towards release. Such movements of the voice give a dynamic prose rhythm in the small, and their relation to each other constitutes a rhythm of the whole. The sequence of accented points in every pair of half-verses in the psalmody is free but not amorphous. Often each hemistich contains two or three accents, and the sequence of these accents, much as the sequence of accents in the opening and closing sections of a measured song-tune, is perceived by both singer and listener as a structural element in the music's motion.

Other elements of archaic ritual singing are also to be observed in these melodies, such as the fitting of many texts with varying numbers of syllables into a few musical formulas, together with the free modification of these polylinear models and alterations in the grouping of little melodic flourishes. Further, ancient synagogal chant has preserved the various ways in which, according to the Bible, the Talmud, Philo, and other sources, the singing was divided among the participants: alternation between leader and congregation, halleluia after each hemistich, antiphony of two half choruses, refrains and terminal verses sung by everybody.

The relationships in form of the psalms with Mesopotamian poetry and those Phoenician or Canaanite poems documented by findings from around 1400 B.C., would indicate connections on the musical side also. In the course of their history the Hebrews absorbed many cultural elements from the active and changing world around them: during their half-nomadic period, after the 13th century in Canaan, where they subjugated an old and wealthy city culture, then in the Babylonian exile, and later, in the Hellenistic period, when they adopted many Greek instruments and Herod the Great (37–4 B.C.) brought in Greek singers. But in its ever new adaptations to the surrounding world and in the purging of foreign influences, Israel grew up to its own greatness and tragedy. Song contributed to the forming of a national and religious self and self-consciousness, notably the songs of triumph of Miriam, Deborah, Judith, or David's lament for Saul and Jonathan.

The change to a new spirituality is shown in the difference between the early prophets and the later. The former had their musical instruments by them and let themselves be inspired by music, even to a state of ecstasy; the latter, on the other hand, carrying on the conflict of Moses with Aaron, strove zealously for a purely spiritual faith and worship: thus did Elijah mock Phoenician priests, who according to archaic custom, called upon their god, and sang to him with loud voices, as though he would hear them with human ears.

The prophets and their successors also exercised severe criticism of secular musical life—Isaiah, for example, who stigmatized voluptuous feasts accompanied by many instruments. But they were not fighting on behalf of the ancient rural folk against the musical life of the cities as such. In ancient Israel farmers, shepherds, and particularly the women, with their dancing and singing, their hand timbrels or tambourines, had indeed represented the song and the music of the whole population. But now the development was directed at freeing the course of yearly festivals from their relationship to work and rural customs and at carrying on Jewish life by means of ritual duties, which were far more difficult to pursue in the country than in the city. Anyone who read in the Holy Scriptures set himself above him "who knows nothing save to talk of oxen," and the time was approaching when strict Jews and Christians were to look upon the unschooled rurals who clung to ancient custom as heathen. It was against the preciousness and luxury of esthetic culture in the musical life of the cities that these reformers turned; they attacked the conduct of the court (the atmosphere around Salomé, for example) and musical urbanity on the model of international Syrian cities like Tyre and Sidon. But they were themselves, like the Christians of the first centuries, city people and representatives of certain strata of urban population.

Individuals, too, and the sects that withdrew into the wilderness, like John the Baptist and his disciples or the Qumran community, stood remote from the rural population proper. But while they turned away from high culture and the capital city of Jerusalem, which appeared to them godless, they brought about by their own decision the decentralization that was bound to take place through the destruction of the Second Temple. The brilliant Temple music inaugurated by the musician-king David and his ostentatious successor Solomon had been the center of the music of monarchic Israel. But now, with the dematerialization and simplification of ritual music, the concrete center in Jerusalem disappeared in favor of a newly conceived, purely spiritual Temple and its music. The simple singing in synagogue and family did not carry on the music of the Temple in its entirety, but perpetuated only a fundamental layer of this many-layered art, transforming it in the new spirit. The period of Israelite temple music was succeeded by the period of synagogal chant that began in the first century A.D.

Roots and Beginnings of the Music of Christendom

Christianity began as a movement within Judaism; hence the Christian service and its singing grew out of Hebraic models, and not out of the high ritual of Jerusalem's Temple with its special characteristics, but out of the lay community's practice which, variously transformed, was carried on also in the provinces and among the reformers. From the Jewish service come, among other things, the horary prayers, the psalms and other biblical songs, as well as several formulas sung by the congregation, like the Alleluia,

Amen, and triple Sanctus. With the texts and their formulas melodic contours must also have been taken over, to be transmitted abroad beyond Palestine—those of them at least that were not entirely local and that were easily spread on account of their archetypical simplicity. That there were such types in the Mediterranean area is certain and is expressly confirmed by Herodotus. A. Z. Idelsohn, Eric Werner, and others have demonstrated the melodic similarity of Gregorian, Armenian, and other Christian chants to those of the Synagogue. Together with the sacred texts various complexes of type and style elements, chiefly psalm formulas and reciting tones, were evidently taken over and preserved (cf. music exx. 9 ff.).

But before the Church had become supranationally powerful and everywhere imposed certain fixed melodies, the original fund of melody could have and must have been altered with the diffusion of Christianity. It would show a lack of method to leave it at a bilateral comparison with synagogal chants, heeding only the connection with these. It is indispensable to draw multilateral comparisons with traditions of all countries in which Christianity established itself. That is difficult, of course, because with the exception of the few known Greek melodies we have no written sources to refer to; but here comparative research in popular traditions is promising, especially since Christian liturgical chant in the first centuries seems to have clung almost throughout to artless popular types. Until such multilateral comparative research makes further progress, general disquisitions on the origins of Christian music as a whole and church music in particular can carry no conviction.

That there must have been a considerable contribution from the Hellenistic period too is indicated by the fact that Christianity at first spread principally to large cities where, chiefly in mission centers like Antioch, Hellenistic culture and language reigned. Thus it took over elements of mystery-cults, Greek words and texts, like Kyrie and Eucharist, motifs in the plastic and pictorial arts, and so forth (cf. also illus. 1). A 3rd-century spiritual song in Greek and with a notated melody has come down to us from Oxyrhynchos in Egypt. The melodic line of the

concluding Amen (a-b-c′-c′-d′-c′/b-g-a-g), which, with variations, occurs four times in the fragment, corresponds with a
widely diffused refrain formula.

Ecclesiastical interdictions and contemporary critical writings
reprove the Christians for still singing heathen tunes and mixing
them with spiritual songs. Besides urban songs, country songs
increasingly mingled in, and, inversely, indigenous popular tunes
became filled with content of Christian meaning. For example, the
jubilus referred to above (p. 37) did not originate exclusively in
the Orient, as has been thought. The Church Fathers, who justify
its use in church when sung without words, speak repeatedly of
the surrounding rural population singing such songs at work, at
harvesting, pasturing their flocks; and they adhere to the pre-
Christian meaning of the Latin word which Sixtus Pompeius
Festus and Terence had defined: *Jubilare est rustica voce incla-
mare* ("*Jubilare* is to sing out loudly with rustic voice"). When
farmers and shepherds became Christians they set Christian texts
to their familiar songs, thereby "baptizing" them, but they would
hardly have learned many unfamiliar melodies in church in order
to sing them outside. This would explain, for example, the comment of St. Jerome (340–420) that the farmer sang Alleluia at
his ploughing: he would certainly not have been singing newly
acquired oriental melodies at his work, but a *jubilus*, usual at
ploughing and as it has come down to us today in backward
regions; only he did not sing it to pagan syllables but to the word
Alleluia (cf. music ex. 15).

Amid all the infiltration and diffusion, however, the germs of
the Gospel proper began to develop. St. Paul exhorted the Colos-
sians: "Let the word of Christ dwell richly in you in all wisdom;
teaching and admonishing one another in psalms and hymns and
spiritual songs, singing with grace in your hearts to the Lord"
(Col. iii, 16). Not purity alone, but plenitude, not only correctitude, but above all love—this was the essential core of the Christian canticle. Without love the best of preachers or singers was
but as sounding brass or a tinkling cymbal. *Cantare amantis est*,
to sing is of the loving, said St. Augustine later.

With the establishment of Christianity in the early Catholic

Church and later as the official religion of State or Empire, ecclesiastical music grew out of old Christian chant. Just as the priest from now on appeared before his community in distinctive liturgical dress, so too church music became differentiated from lay singing. In this process it grew away from those beginnings it had had in common with synagogal chant. Developing into a sacred art with high and pontifical Masses, it took on characteristics similar to those of the music of yore in the Temple at Jerusalem.

A Glance at the Liturgical Chant of Eastern Christianity

When Christianity spread around the Mediterranean basin, East and West were linked through strong contacts in culture, language (the cultivation of church Latin began in the 2nd century), and Rome's imperial administration. In the following centuries a great many things happened in world history that contributed to the breaking up of this unity: the fitful separations of the Byzantine Empire from the Roman (4th century); the invasion of the West by the Huns (410); the expansion of Islam beginning in the 7th century; the crowning of Charlemagne as Emperor of the Holy Roman Empire (800), which made official the separation of the two empires; and, most immediate to our present subject, the schism of 1054 between the Roman Catholic Church and the Orthodox. Since the beginnings of the Byzantine Empire many forces had been working towards the separate development of Christianity in the East and the West and of the rites of the Eastern and Western Churches. In this process connections in the field of liturgical music were also loosened.

In the West the development took place that led to the special position of occidental music. In the East, after its initial spread to Asia Minor and North Africa, Christianity was pushed aside by Islam. But at first, in the great day of Syrian hymnology and the glory of Byzantium, the East was in many respects superior to the West in both liturgy and music and had a strong influence on it. A study of the East should therefore also throw much light upon the musical history of the West.

Such a study is also important because the East produced a great variety of styles in liturgical melody that were independent and of some worth in themselves. While in the West Gregorian chant was everywhere enforced after the Carolingian period, in the East quite different stores of melodies continued to exist side by side. Although, for example, Russian liturgical chant shows a Byzantine origin in its texts and terminology, the melodic treasure it has transmitted is of an entirely different sort.

Furthermore, Eastern Christian chant is important for the universal history of music because it forms an invaluable source for discovering the common roots and origins of all Christian music. Unlike the Gregorian, it is to be found not only in extensive written material but also in oral traditions that have preserved stylistic elements from Antiquity. Pre-Christian elements have survived among the Coptic Christians of Egypt and Ethiopia; the various sound implements that accompany the chant in their church services include little bells and sistra that go back to ancient Egyptian instruments. In Syrian, Armenian, and other Eastern churches that lively prose rhythm still exists which we have met in synagogal chant (cf. p. 91). Differences between long and short values were also written down, for instance in the Armenian notation. In the Neo-Greek heritage of Byzantine chant, for example, one is struck by the principle of syllabic connection, which is to be distinguished from the free filling up by weak or unaccented beats, the condensing and the rational subdividing of rhythmic values. If one verse of a hymn has more syllables than the preceding, the quarter notes are not subdivided into two eighths or three triplets, but further quarter notes are added which, however, fit into the rhythm of the whole without interrupting it. The adding on and leaving off of syllables accords with the elastic extensibility and contractibility of the whole rhythmic pattern.

The music of the Byzantine Empire had an important part in court and church ceremonial and hence in the gilded lustre of that Empire in which something of the divine kingdom of archaic cultures still lived. In contrast to the official clergy, there were now also cloistered communities, in whose calm and passionless existence we may also see some heritage from the Stoics.

This traditionalism of Byzantine music is particularly evident in its principle of creating no new melodies but instead variously grouping, abbreviating, or expanding formulas organized in four authentic and four plagal modes (*echoi*). Similarly Byzantine music theory was concerned not with progressive conquering of new problems but with learned preservation of its antique heritage. For universal history, which must study not only the substance but also the forms of evolution, such traditionalist attitudes are of the greatest interest. They contrast sharply with the ideologies and accomplishments of occidental progress and of modern avantgardism.

THE FURTHER COURSE OF
DEVELOPMENT IN THE ORIENT

If, despite such enormous differences as there are between Arabian and Chinese music, one contrasts the great oriental cultures as a whole with the West and its music, one must confess to taking a European perspective; yet there is also an objective ground for so doing. None of those cultures, before turning to the global industrial civilization of today, went through the historical evolution owing to which Western music brought about its own special age, the Third Age of music, and prepared the Fourth Age. None of them perfected or spread a musical notation as a general basis; none of them became a culture with written music. Hence they did not elaborate fixed musical compositions in score, nor did they create artistic structures in polyphony or architectonics; there is no oriental counterpart to fugue or symphony.

They are therefore not subject to historical study to the same extent as the West, and we cannot reconstruct their musical history upon so large and solid a series of musical manuscripts, editions, or other dated sources.

This conclusion is by no means deprecatory. The oriental civilizations too are "immediate to God." They developed so much that is original and important that their contribution to the universal history of music should be thoroughly explored. It is regrettable that the present volume must be restricted to a brief survey.

Conceptions about Music
                              In all oriental cultures four successive layers are to be distinguished. First, they were rooted in prehistoric and primitive times, from which they retained much: China, for example, with its important heritage from the Megalithic period. Secondly, they were modified by the ancient high civilizations that came into being around 3000 B.C. Thirdly, they were influenced by Greek Antiquity, especially by the Hellenistic period with its music theory and other achievements, and by the spread of Christianity; what survived of Antiquity in the East followed a development different from that in the West, but no less fundamental. Fourthly, each of these cultures built its own individuality upon the base laid by this triple heritage, and in course of time each enjoyed active relations with the rest and an interchange of influences. Of special import was the expansion of the great religions—Buddhism and a thousand years later, Islam—which brought with them a wide diffusion of musical elements.

These manifold roots and layers must not be lost sight of if one wishes to achieve a historical picture of the music of the Orient. Thus in the history of ideas underlying conceptions about music one must look beyond the commonplaces of "the ancient wisdom of the East" and "cult and magic in the music of the ancient Orient" to distinguish various ideas that came up at various times, were diffused to a limited extent, and often antagonistic to each other. An example of such tensions and hostilities is offered by the violent attacks of Chuang-tse upon Confucianism on the one hand and on the other upon the ascetic tendency of Mo-Ti. From a sociological point of view also it is to be remembered that the countless speculations and symbolic interpretations do not represent the view of the whole people, but for the most part only those of an intellectual elite or particular class. This is borne out by Li-Ji when he says: "The animals, indeed, know sound, but not tone, and the masses, indeed, know tone but not music. Only the noble person is capable of understanding the meaning of music."

In India and China, furthermore, as in Greece, the word music had various meanings; in older writings it includes also dance and poetry: so, for example, various aphorisms of Confucius are to be interpreted. Also as in Grecian traditions many miraculous stories about music and the rules for its magic use were current but not everywhere accepted. If even among the primitive peoples the charm of music had a power beyond magic, this is evidence of a more exalted concept reaching from magic into poetry. Oriental poetry is full of most beautiful examples of such poetic sublimation. In a poem in the Shu-king, the earliest Chinese chronicle, Kwei, the director of music, says: "I strike the sounding stone lightly and strongly./ I touch the harp and zither gently/ to singing. Then fathers and ancestors draw near:/ they sit as guests at the royal feast . . . Pan-flutes and bells with their resonance,/ these alternate with the song. Then birds and beasts press forward/ and to the sound of holy music/ the phoenix pair soars festively round about."

In the Middle Ages it was a familiar conception that *musica mundana* (harmony in the macrocosm), *musica humana* (harmony in the microcosm, i.e. man), and *musica instrumentalis* (practical music) had an analogous structure. This view was nurtured and modified also in the Orient. To an understanding of one of its most important modifications, its determination by astrological and cosmological considerations, some ideas of Arnold Gehlen may be helpful. Man gladly lets the external world take over the direction of his own actions. "Hence the remarkable fascination of automatism, of the regular rotation he first became aware of in the heavens, and of the monotony of the eternal return: this awakens a resonance in his own pulse, and, inversely, he feels his own action being carried along in the lines of force of the revolving world and of Nature's rhythms." Surely the euphoric effect of music rests largely upon "our deep tie with rhythmic, periodic, automatic processes of the external world." Such ideas are more elemental than the formalizing of musical and cosmological notions into schemata coordinating the steps of the scale with different dimensions of heaven and earth, or the comparisons drawn by lovers of analogy that equate the tonic with the ruler, the supertonic with the minister.

In addition, concepts and emotional reactions inspired by the irrational and dynamic in music and in the world were active. Indian metaphysics thought of the essence of music as the primal impersonal force that Schopenhauer called the "Will," the common source of all germination, vital force, desire. The Brahma of the Vedas, identified in the Upanishads with atman (soul), was held to be the primal force that flows through everything in the world; the expression "Brahma" for this force, which was in the beginning and is forever active, at first meant song, the sung formula, the word. Lao-tse expressed the nature of human music and celestial music in another way: "Being in unison with men is human music, and being in unison with God is celestial music. Whoever understands celestial music in life remains in accord with Nature and in death takes part in the process of transformation of things . . . Equanimity and rest are principles that move through heaven and earth and all creation. That is celestial music. Celestial music is that with which the wise man nourishes all living things."

The concept of ethos that was particularly widespread in ancient China is also expressive of views and experiences more elemental and on a higher level than formalization and fairytales. Chuang-tse asks, what is a noble person? "He who conducts himself in accord with the principles of humanity, accomplishing good deeds, following the rule of righteousness, observing good manners in his bearing, expressing a sense of harmony through music and thereby becoming kind and compassionate."

Thus the oriental view of music embraces many and various

ideas: heterogeneous and common to humanity, ascetic and devoutly vital, rigid in form and elemental, extrovert and introvert. It is multicolored and multiform. Amid its confusion of voices one hears the deep tones of metaphysical mysticism. "Great space has no corners," says Lao-tse, "great gifts take long to ripen, great music is gently heard . . . And the Tao is hidden." Tao is the way, the truth, the cosmic order.

Maqam and Raga

There are no oriental musical compositions that have passed, like the poems of Hafiz or Li Tai-pe, into world literature, nor any composers known as are these poets. But before the influx of Western music there had been no musical compositions written down to be exactly reproduced, only a collection of melodies more or less fixed, and over and above these, certain melodic types on which the player molded his performance. Such types consist of melodic formulas, mostly within a given tonality. Each has a name, a character, and often too a place in the order of the daily hours and the seasons. To the practical musician it provides a guideline and at the same time a frame for the play of improvisation. Hence it is not like a Platonic idea, but represents a superpersonal living spirit that comes and goes. It is not as defined as an individual piece of music and not as general as a genre, but lies somewhere between the two. It might best be compared to certain types of composition, like the aria of opera seria. It is distinguished from folk-song types particularly by its conceptual approach and its set limits.

An Arabic *maqam* is determined in the first instance by its tonality, but also by fixed melodic formulas and direction, as well as by its emotional character and the aura or nimbus that accrues to it through its use and its function. In India several terms were used for the various scales and modes but not always and everywhere with the same meaning: *murchana* (a mode of more specific nature than the *grama* scale, from which it was derived), *jati*, *raga*. The jati—according to Bharata (2nd century B.C.), some chapters in whose great work on drama, the *Nâṭyaśâstra*, are our oldest source of information about Indian music—had its own final tone, cadence tones, extent, typical turns, etc. The name raga (from *ranj*, to color) indicates primarily emotional value, the effect on the soul. Hence tempo and style of execution, as well as chromatic alterations and typical flourishes, gave the raga its character.

A richly symbolical way of thought and a soaring imagination endowed maqams and ragas with the most varied qualities. Strange stories were told of what dreadful things would happen if a raga intended for a given hour were played at another hour; furthermore, melody types were personified and depicted as divine or human beings. Arnold Bake points out that this development took several centuries; the first pictorial representations of a raga are not found before the 16th century, and southern India did not join in this development. Bake quotes a passage that says: "Ragas should be sung at the right time, as the ancient rules prescribe. But if the king commands it, they may be sung at any time, and in this case the singer need not adhere to the right time."

Certain psychic qualities and influences were also attributed to the Arabic maqams, but different ones by different authors. The position is evidently similar to that of the ethical doctrine of the Greeks. Around the real characteristics resting on the form and use of a melody type, speculations and fables were intertwined, creating an atmosphere of fantasy. Learned writers in our time repeat such fables as though they had always been taken seriously or indeed even gave proof that the conception of music in Antiquity and the Orient was only and always magical.

"Exotic" Scales and Styles

Our view of the music of the Orient has been distorted by hackneyed misrepresentations. Many an author describes it as a collection of artificial tonal systems, forced, unnatural vocalizings, with guttural tones, falsettos, embellishments, over-refined rhythms. But in fact these special exotic traits do not amount to general characteristics. In the Orient also the artificial is mixed with the natural, the universally human.

On the one hand, favored by the prevailing use of monophony, various types of ornamental melos have evolved. The cities of the Near East are particularly fond of singing in crinkly melodic lines, with vibrating voice, augmented seconds, and a lot of mannerisms. Brilliant virtuosity is displayed in coloratura singing as well as on the drum and in the playing of flute, vina, lute, and other melody instruments. Polyrhythms and complicated measures are especially widespread in India, Turkey, and various Near East countries.

But over against tendencies to artificial refinement there stand the simpler "natural orders" which, stemming from primitive and early times, governed popular music in the high cultures and among their neighbor peoples. Theory still builds on the foundation laid by the Greeks. In China classic simplicity has reigned since earliest times with symmetrical four-beat measure and semitoneless pentatonicism.

The "Oriental" does not hear differently from the "European"; that prejudice is absurd in view of the great contrasts within the Orient itself. Furthermore, those styles that are distinct from the structures common to primitive peoples, Antiquity, and Western music are far more localized than those that adhere to these norms; and they originated not from some entirely different ground but through refinement and alteration of general and more natural forms. This is demonstrated in rhythm, line, and form and also in the realm where it is most difficult, the tonal systems.

Tonal systems based on consonances hold exclusive sway in large parts of Asia, particularly North Asia, Mongolia and China, and partial sway in all the rest. These are the tetratonic, the semitoneless pentatonic, and the seven-tone diatonic scales that correspond with the Greek and medieval modes. The primitive heritage has lived on in popular music: in Indo-China, for example, children sing archaic triadic melodies, boatmen archaic tetratonic tunes. The same universally human characteristics as elsewhere determine the music of women, children, and rural populations in the Orient also.

Those singular systems, however, which differentiate oriental from European music diverge less from recognized harmonic orders than a onesided view of different or exotic matter is likely to admit. Unlike the new music of our century, the Orient has developed no theory that would account for stylistic elements so different from those of Greek theory and lay another foundation for them. Even Arabic music theory starts with the three principal consonances and the simple numerical relations resulting from them. There is no "exotic" music theory radically different from ours.

Similarly, there is in practice no system that has not at least the octave as its framing interval. For the most part the fifth and fourth belong to the structure, even in the Orient. Where polyphony extends beyond a differentiated monophony, for example in tones occurring together on rhythmic accents, the chief consonances take precedence. Deviations from the normal harmonic structure (pentatonicism with semitones, Gipsy scales, augmented fourths, raising or lowering of a step) are chiefly to be understood as nuances and coloration, as both Robert Lachmann and Jacques Handschin have shown. Musicians and listeners usually have the simpler form in their ears so that they can appreciate and enjoy odd divergencies as an added charm. It is naive to think that quarter tones, in the sense of precisely measured microtones, seem just as natural to all Arabic musicians and their average listeners, as major and minor and the triad seem to the European.

Third-century China already possessed a system of 12 semitones. But this was only a collection or reservoir of naturally occurring tones, not used as a proper chromatic scale. In practice, music moved along five- or seven-tone scales, using one degree or another as fundamental. It would be the same thing as if we played the piano in only pentatonic and major scales, but now in C major, now in C♯ major. Even in the medieval church modes B and B♭ both occur, though not as melodic intervals; similarly in Japan, India, and the Near East tones occur with their inflections, which are used, however, only in the sense of alternatives.

Nor are the systems formed of intervals smaller than the semitone used as scales. Thus Indian theory reckons with 22 śruti to the octave as the smallest values (as in rhythm with the smallest units of duration) but builds no melodies out of successions of such instances. The number 22 was not arrived at by mathematical division of the octave; instead, according to Bharata, starting from a diatonic scale of seven steps, the great whole tone (approximately a major second) was divided into four śruti, the small whole tone (approximately a minor second) into three, the semitone into two, thus reaching the number 22. Robert Lachmann has established that one step smaller than a semitone is rarely followed by another in Indian practice, never in Arabo-Islamic music. In so far even the Arabic quarter-tone system has only theoretical significance and is far removed from the quarter-tone music of the 20th century.

Rather special are the tempered scales widely used in Indonesia and Siam, in which the octave is divided into five or seven equal distances. The physiological capacity of the ear may also come into play here, perceiving equal distances, if not as values quite as acute as the consonances, still as approximately equal. Yet these scales are not founded exclusively upon the principle of distance as others are on consonance and the relationship of tones. The fact of starting with the octave, as well as the division into five or seven steps, already indicates that these tempered systems rest upon the "more natural" orders of *Gestalt* psychology; more will be said of this in the section on Indonesia. We can see by Javanese song-tunes, says Curt Sachs, "that the Javanese musician hardly feels any differently from the European." When such melodies were played in the Javanese tempered system, the deviations could in part be tolerated by the ear, in part enjoyed as nuances; as yet no sufficient study has been made of this question from the music-psychological angle. In any case, the equidistant systems in the Orient have by far not the same importance, diffusion, or originality as those founded upon harmony.

In view of the fact, recently emphasized by Heinrich Husmann, that European instruments, such as recorders, are often out of tune by as much as a quarter of a tone and even more, we must reckon with the "tolerance" of many musicians and listeners also in the

Orient. It is therefore questionable whether many of these extraordinary scales are intentional, actually "willed." On out-of-tune pianos or carillons playing European folk tunes scales acoustically just as odd are produced, but these are random products and not scales in the same sense as a major scale or a church mode, which is objective, a norm with historical reality. A scale is not the sum of the steps arranged on any chance instrument, but an ideal norm that listeners as well as players have in mind—not primarily an empiric fact but a "rule" as medieval authors define it.

India

Of all the oriental high cultures that extend into the present the Indian is the oldest, for the Indus civilization in which it roots goes back, like the related Sumerian, to about 3000 B.C. It was, indeed, so much destroyed by the Aryan invasion of around 1500 that but little of it remains. But if one compares one of the surviving fragments, the torso of a dancing God from the 3rd millennium B.C., with some dancing Shiva of more recent times, say of the 12th century A.D., one constant fundamental motif of Indian art and music appears: the deification of the vital force and its cycle.

The period of the Veda, the sacred lore, and of the Vedic writings—namely the songs and sayings (Vedas), the sacrificial rituals (Brahmanas), the doctrine of the unity of the human self with its original divine cause (Upanishads)—lasted from 1500 to 300. The word Brahma stems from magic ritual and originally stood for the magic power of ritual chant; in highly developed metaphysical theology, however, it came to mean the primal force manifesting itself in the voice, in storm, in fire and other forms. It was presently equated with atman (breath, seat of all life). "He who living in the voice is yet different from the voice, whom the voice knows not, whose body is the voice, who guides the voice from inside, that is your atman, your secret guide, the immortal." Similarly it is said of the eye: "He who living in the eye is yet different from the eye . . . ," and of the ear, of heat, of intelligence, of the seed, of the individual self. With the ideal sound "om" and meditation upon it, say these texts, Vedic melodies lead to the world of Brahma. Some picture of the ritual music of ancient India is best achieved by comparing orally transmitted traditional tunes with the oldest layers of Jewish, Christian, and other cultic chant. The hymns of the Rigveda are chanted in archaic recitative formulas of very limited range, much like those also known from Western chant (cf. music ex. 11).

A third period came about on the one hand through the birth of Buddhism in the 6th century B.C.—that extreme reaction against the Indian cult of the vital force—which later, however, disappeared almost completely in India, and on the other through a long succession of invasions as well as influences from the West. With the spread of Hellenistic culture, Greek music theory also found its way to India, where it was characteristically transformed: mathematical logic lost its significance while classification and symbolic attributions came to the fore. From abroad, too, came most of the musical instruments, some during Antiquity, some with the spread of Islam and Arabic culture.

Again and again the Indian mind, and with it Hinduism, triumphed over foreign influences. Old forms were cultivated as classical music, and old views about music were maintained, animated, transformed. In the 13th century A.D., when in Europe too great compendia of musical theory (*Summa Musicae*) were being put forth or opening new ways, the Brahman Sārngadeva wrote a voluminous book, which he called *The Ocean of Music*. He conceives Brahma, the primal creative principle, to be song not manifest, not perceptible to the senses, and presents music as the way to salvation and to union with Brahma.

In the following centuries the advance of Islam and the Mongolian invasion brought matters to a split between North and South as well as between the Moslem and the Hindu areas of India. Music as an art became exclusive to the court and an elite of connoisseurs who were supposed—according to a current phrase—to be "of the same heart" as the musicians. In this milieu high forms of virtuosity and coloratura singing, tonal refinement and subtletly of rhythm were promoted. They do not represent the music of India as a whole, but rather a lofty peak, the culmination of a multiplicity of styles corresponding to the various social layers and racial groupings of this subcontinent.

Indonesia

Indian culture belongs preponderantly to the Near East, Indonesian culture on the whole to the Far East. In the former, chamber music with stringed instruments and hand drums prevails, in the latter, in Java and in Bali, orchestral music with metallophones and idiophones. Only the music that attains to a high-culture level in these two islands will be briefly considered here. But there are also in Indonesia, which is one of the earliest parts of the earth to have been inhabited by human beings, primitive peoples of the most varied sorts. Today's Polynesians once settled there, before their astonishing capacity for seafaring had brought them to the Pacific Islands. They employ a polyphony far exceeding elementary forms, as well as introvert dances in which, now seated, now standing, often, as in certain Hindu dances, only the arms, hands, and head move. For Indonesia too such interiorized dances are characteristic; they are midway between dance with the whole body and the dance of the soul that is pure music.

In Java during the first millennium of our era the spread of Indian culture bore fruit: here stands the greatest monument of Buddhist architecture and sculpture, the huge temple of Borobudur, "the many Buddhas." The island later fell under Arabic influence, and after the 16th century under the domination of the Portuguese and then of the Dutch. Bali, on the contrary, kept much freer of Buddhist and Arabic interference; it retained Hinduism and, in its orchestral art, the music of ancient Chinese ritual.

Like most oriental music, that of the gamelan was transmitted by oral tradition until a few decades ago. We know of neither notation nor any theoretical writings; but Indonesian music theory—to which the Greek term "theory" can be only conditionally applied—has been orally transmitted and thus offers us something to go on in picturing the pre-theoretical theory of early high cultures.

The tonal systems in use here are consequently empirical in character rather than based on principle. They are not constructed, not derived from the cycle of fifths, from harmonic division of strings, or from other scholarly theoretical traditions and their applications. Contrary to earlier views—in which the joy of discovery exaggerated the basic significance of exotic traits—more recent studies (by Mantle Hood, Laurence Picken, and others) have established that slendro and pelog are not equidistant systems throughout, i.e. their octaves are not divided into respectively 5 or 7 intervals of equal size. Their customary modes are differentiated by their tonal structure (location of tonic and dominant) as well as by characteristic cadences. They furthermore point out parallels with ancient Chinese cadence formulas and entire melodies; which reinforces the probability previously suggested by von Hornbostel and others that the semitoneless pentatonic scales underlie the tempered systems. The tuning of ancient instruments dug up in Java, as well as Indonesian folk music, also indicate that tetratonic and pentatonic scales preceded these systems. Javanese children sing in semitoneless pentatonic.

This whole culture, furthermore, shows a tendency to the stylization of tones. Even the country folk modify their scale steps according to these systems. Women singing to the accompaniment of the gamelan cultivate a pinched and nasal vocal quality and melodies with glissandos and coloratura. In the orchestra, variety of dynamics, agogics, and tone-color contrasts with regularity of rhythm and strophic sequence.

The heterophony of the gamelan has no relation to what Plato called heterophony, but it is one of the finest forms of orchestral polyphony, and, together with Japanese traditions especially, offers us an idea of what the ancient orchestral art of the Far East, now vanished, may have been like. The instruments have different functions: kettle-shaped brass gongs and metallophones with bamboo resonators carry the melody in long, regular values; xylophones and metallophones without resonators, hence with shorter tones, break up the tune into smaller values; flute and rebab (the Arabo-Persian spike fiddle) wind about and soar above them, sometimes playing a real countermelody; gongs reinforce the accents of rhythm and form, like sonorous punctuation marks.

China

The Middle Kingdom was the central country of the Far East in music also. Its culture radiated not only to Indonesia but also to Farther India, Korea, Japan. It was not, however, the center or original country of Eurasia as a whole, especially not in the period of the first high civilizations. At that time, in the 3rd millennium B.C., the far-eastern parts of Eurasia, like the far-western, still lay on the periphery of these civilizations. Contrary to a fabulous tradition that must have sprung up much later, Chinese high culture does not enter the light of history until about 1500 B.C., and even from around 1000 we as yet know no more types of instruments than the sounding stones and a ball-shaped flute.

In these sounding stones, however, a fundamental characteristic of Far-Eastern music, and of Chinese music in particular, already appears: the predilection for idiophones. Perhaps it corresponds with the special relation of Chinese art to Nature; the surrender in ever-attentive listening to the direct resonance of wood or stone, to the life of the material itself, has been described by Werner Danckert. Indicative of this quality is also the later grouping of instruments according to the material of which they are made: stone, wood, bamboo, gourd, metal, and so forth.

Enduring ideas in the Chinese conception of music came to birth in the great period of the philosophers around Confucius and Lao-tse. Like their contemporaries in Greece and the Prophets in Israel, these men were not so much exponents of the existing folk mind, but rather monitors and guides to new beliefs and new customs. The polemics in their discourses and their writings reveal the contradictions in various positions and tendencies in those times. Yet these may well have been connected with various positions and tendencies in other times. Hence one should seek to understand the ideas of these philosophers as they related to their particular epoch and also as they reflected more general types of music.

"The playing of the noble person," says Confucius, "is sweet and gentle, it keeps an equable disposition, enlivens and stimulates. He does not nourish in his heart moods of pain and mourning, defiant and violent movements are unknown to his body. The playing of the common man is different: it is loud and fast, then again moribund and vague, the reflection of a brutal spirit of death. His heart is not tempered to harmonious balance, gentle and pleasing movements are unknown to his body." Moderation and calm are also fundamental motifs of the genial philosopher and poet Chuang-tse, who in another respect turned against Confucius, questioning his doctrine that human society and manners should be kept in order through ceremonial and music. Following Lao-tse he teaches that assiduous moralizing only confuses things and goes against their original nature. The leaning towards esthetic differentiation and nuance also makes for confusion. "People with over-acute hearing confuse the five tones and exaggerate the differences in tone of the six pitch pipes and the differences in timbre of metals, stones, strings, and bamboo, of the Huang-chung [the yellow bell, the fundamental that "begot" all other tones] and the Ta-lü. Is it not so? Such a one was Shi-khuang, the music master." Just as in making music too subtle, insists Chuang-tse, in taking an ascetic attitude towards it one is acting against the nature of things and of human beings. Mo Ti "wrote the treatise 'against music' and taught that one 'should be sparing. Do not sing in life and do not mourn in death.' " Mo Ti, continues Chuang-tse, taught all-embracing love, the principle of doing good to all men, and he preached against war. "He wished to do away with the ceremonial and the music of the Ancients . . . But what sort of teaching is it then that forbids one to sing when one wants to sing, to weep when one wants to weep, and to enjoy music when one feels happy? It allows people to live strenuously and die miserably and is surely all too severe. It makes people sad and sour-tempered and is in practice difficult to follow. That does not seem to me to be the teaching of the wise. For it is against human nature and only the few can endure it. Even if Mo Ti himself could carry out this doctrine, how is it with the great majority of men? If a doctrine departs from humanity in general, it must be regarded as far from the way that sets the world in order."

Confucius (551–479) was younger than Zarathustra and a contemporary of Buddha, Pythagoras, and Heraclitus. Chuang-tse died around 275 B.C., at the beginning of the Hellenistic period. During the Han Dynasty (206 B.C.–220 A.D.) after severe wars, internal struggle for power, and much devastation, the Chinese Empire was made over from a feudal into a bureaucratic state. As in Egypt at about the same time, salvation was sought in the restoration of archaic rites and a state control of culture. An Imperial Bureau of Music was set up, charged with watching over and regulating the entire musical life. The effort to re-establish the good order of a far distant epoch naturally led to utopian ideas about the past and a tendency to transfer later ideas back into that "golden age." This applies for example to the fixation of an absolute pitch and rhythmic norms. Cosmological speculation, too, about the harmony of heaven, earth, and man and its application to music theory had more ancient roots, as we already know, but now for the first time was made into a rigid system of regulations—and probably not without influence from the West.

Pictures of musicians, jugglers, and women dancers show that even in this epoch of restoration musical life did not yield entirely to the doctrinaire insistence of scholars and officials. Western influences in these and the following centuries brought with them various instruments, like the lute and harp, and apparently also theater with music. From India Buddhism was transplanted to the Far East and made connections of its own with indigenous religions, for example in Tibet.

From the interplay of Western influences with native talents Chinese culture came to its period of finest flowering, the Tang period. It lasted from the 7th to the 9th century, more or less contemporary with the first centuries of Islam and the Carolingian period. China now became a world power and its international metropolis the greatest city in the world. Virtuosos and orchestras from India, Turkestan, Tibet, Mongolia, and other countries met here. Compositions they performed included the suite; we have a manuscript of an orchestral suite of eight movements in different tempos, though its notation has not yet been deciphered. A great variety of musical languages, styles, and colors worked side by side here, were interwoven. Precious instruments and fine pictures of music-making women give us a clue to the high esthetic level of culture enjoyed by the upper classes of society.

A main motif in lyric poetry of this period is the sound of a solitary instrument in the midst of natural surroundings. Poets speak of the plaintive flute upon a watchtower or the sounding of a bell amid nocturnal rain. In the quivering vibrancy of the lute they hear the wind through frost, "the song of olden times, that people of our day hardly understand." Quite alone in a bamboo thicket Wang Wei the poet gently touches the strings; only the moon comes to join, to understand him. His gift of thanks to a superintendent of the court closes with the lines:

> Thou askest, is life worth living—
> O hark!: the song of the fisherman across the sands . . .

After this period, so open to the surrounding world and to such a variety of styles, the Sung period (960–1279) withdrew into more specifically Chinese attitudes and styles. A few sketches of ritual and secular melodies that have come down to us may date from the 12th century or later. It is a difficult but necessary and rewarding task to ferret out the chronology of unwritten traditions. In this, one must also consider the traditions of various neighboring lands and draw conclusions about the common roots of all these from comparison with various backward areas. Thus from Indonesia and other Eastern countries light is shed upon ancient Chinese ritual music. In Japan, both court-music traditions and certain old music notebooks may provide sources for finding out what were the accomplishments and effects of the Tang epoch.

In the 13th century, from which for the first time the text of a Chinese drama has been transmitted to us, a type of drama with singing and orchestra was developed. Further types of music in the theater came into being from the Ming period (14th–17th centuries) on, leading to Chinese opera, which still continues today. In the 16th century appeared the great work in which Prince Tsai-yü offers a general picture of the music of ancient China. On the whole, the modern era, which in the West has been a period of rapid development, has been less fruitful for China and other oriental countries than their own bygone times of efflorescence.

Japan

Japanese music differs from the Chinese music of more recent times in greater freedom and color of rhythm, polyphony, tonality. In it too pentatonicism predominates, but a pentatonic with semitones in various positions and hence in various tonalities (for example e'-c'-b-a-f-e) and with modulation from one tonality to another. In these features, which diverge from the newer Chinese styles, certain older stylistic elements that once were also current in China have been preserved, but they have also been stamped with an expression characteristic of Japan, the same expression by which she turned Buddhism into Zen Buddhism and adapted Chinese influences in her pictorial and plastic arts.

The flowering of Japanese art and music began in the 8th century, yet certain sources also testify to a developed musical life in the preceding centuries, for example the report of the despatch of a great Korean orchestra in 453 A.D. to the funeral ceremonies for the Emperor (Korea had been subjected to Japan since the 4th century), or the following 7th-century poem to the zither, which carries on an ancient poetic motif:

Koto, scarcely touched, sounds in tones of lament.
Could it be, that under the koto's wood, the loved one lives?

In the 7th century Japan became a centralized bureaucratic state and as in China some centuries before an Office of Music was installed at the imperial court in 702. It was charged with the cultivation of certain traditions and the regulating and supervising of the education of court musicians. In the Heian epoch (794–1192) that court music was developed which is still nurtured today as a classical heritage; it is called *Gagaku*, fine, genteel music, and includes besides orchestral and dance music both older and newer song. The music to accompany dancing is called *Bugaku.*

An informative source for the Heian epoch and the following times is the contemporary chronicle of Tachibana Narisūe, completed in 1254. He describes performances at court and mentions that the emperor himself sometimes took part on the flute. Occasionally disputes arose over the correct interpretation of a piece, or one musician would criticize another: "Och, but he plays without devotion! When he plays one feels nothing." As in Chinese lyrics, the theme of solitary music amid nature is much savored: we have an account of how a distinguished Japanese traveler played the *biwa* (lute) under a big tree before an inn "all night long, totally absorbed." Characteristic also is genteel society's poetical playing with its heritage of mythical motifs. When in the early light of dawn towards the end of a party the company looks about to see whether grasses and trees will actually dance when a certain piece is played, someone calls out: "Indeed, they seem to be dancing!" and is applauded for his observation; someone else protests that "they're just stirring in the morning breeze," but everybody laughs at him and pities him for being so uneducated, so unpoetical.

An ancient heritage still in favor today is the Nô play, a lyric choral drama molded by Zen Buddhism and in some of its characteristic features related to ancient Greek drama. Limited to few dramatis personae and a chorus, it consists of cultic dances, recitatives, and antiphonal singing. The melodies standing out from the recitatives consist of variations on only nine formulas. The accompanying orchestra consists of various kinds of stick-beaten and hand-beaten drums together with a single transverse flute. Other melodic instruments are lacking, and even the flute has only a few formulas to play. Both vocal and instrumental parts are set down in musical script. Notations were developed particularly in the 13th and 15th centuries, for the fixing of Buddhist liturgical chant. During modern times, as in China and Europe, various types of theater music came into being, like the puppet theater and the popular dance-drama *kanda-matsūr*. Furthermore there developed music for the two chief instruments of the newer Japan: from the 16th century on, for the *shamisen*, a long-necked guitar with three strings, and from the 17th, for the *koto* (zither). From the 17th century until 1868 Japan purposely closed its doors to foreign influences, but in the last hundred years has opened them to the new Age more widely than almost any other country of the Orient.

The Arabo-Islamic Culture Area

In the 7th century, about the same time as the civilization of Western Christianity was becoming established, Arabo-Islamic culture came into being. It too was rooted in Judeo-Christian spiritualized representation of the Divinity and dematerialization of divine service, and in the rationalism of Greek Antiquity as well. It too, a late culture, entered upon a complex heritage and nevertheless began afresh in many respects with a strong sense of mission and the power to achieve supernational expansion. The two cultures had much in common, yet were in many ways opposed; for an understanding of both it is instructive to compare them.

Pre-Islamic Arabia was not altogether restricted to the nomadic Bedouin way, but belonged to the border regions of early high cultures. The origin of Arab music lay not simply in the recitative-like singing of camel-drivers but also in the women's songs and dances of that Megalithic urban culture from which Islam took the Kaaba and simultaneously with it certain influences from Syria and Mesopotamia, the ancient centers of the Near East. The Arabs so much the more came to adopt the musical traditions of Syria, and of a Persia re-invigorated under the Sassanids, when they conquered those countries. They spread among populations that were much more deeply saturated with ancient civilization than the West European peoples of that time, and accordingly the rise of their culture was much more rapid. By the time of the Carolingians their big cities, from Bagdad to Cordova, were among the most brilliant in the world.

The international musical language we call Arabic music spread to Spain and to North India and Indonesia, in the process superimposing itself upon the native music of the various peoples of these regions and remodeling it. Universal in its basic elements, it became differentiated, according to the distinctive characters of the conquered countries especially, into a Western style-area of Andalusian character and a Near-East style-area with Egyptian and Syrian, Persian, and later, Turkish centers. The official ritual chant of Islam is everywhere the same in its simple recitative formulas, while its richer melodic cantillation differs from mosque to mosque. The folk music of the different countries and the musical art of the cultivated Arab classes had less connection with each other than folk and art music in the West, yet many a ruler, like the Caliph Harun-al-Rashid, liked to hear what the people were singing or had his musicians play it for him.

Iconoclastic Islam, even more than early Christianity and the Reformation of Calvin and Zwingli, was shaped by puristic tendencies the radical zealots of which sought to eliminate music altogether, while even their moderate supporters so restricted it that Islam never did arrive at as rich an unfolding of its religious music as the Catholic or Lutheran Churches. In the reading of the Koran the love of music could find expression only to the extent that the reading was preferably confided to beautiful voices. More melodious are the calls to prayer sounded several times a day by the muezzin from high on a minaret. Religious chant pervaded the entire life of Mohammedan communities; and solemn processions and pilgrimages, during which tunes of pagan origin were also sung, were accompanied by pipes, trumpets, and drums. Certain sects too, cultivated music as a way to ecstasy and of penetrating to the core of the soul and of the world. Such was the case with the whirling dervishes, whose founder and Mevlana, the Persian poet and mystic Jelaladdin Rumi, begins his great didactic work with the verses:

Listen to the reed flute, what it is proclaiming,
Listen to its plaint, aflame with nostalgic sorrow:
When they cut me off by the reed-rimmed lake
The whole world wept at my woe.

"The melodies," he goes on to say, "are filled with the fervor of love and the longing for reunion of that which has been separated."

In rebellion against their interdiction, wine and song are praised and glorified in many verses like these of Ibn Cosman, an Arabian poet of the 12th century, living in Spain:

And the singer is excellent,
And the flute plays so sweetly—
And the heavens pure and radiant,
And the wine so bright and clear!

Soon after the capital had been moved from Medina to Damascus, the courts became centers for the cultivation of secular music. Many rulers, like the ancient oriental princes, had countless women singers, dancers, and musicians in their harems; some were enthusiastic music lovers and patrons of music, while others adhered to a puristic sobriety.

Arab culture has a predilection for solo and chamber music. Biographical appreciations of several performing and creative musicians have come down to us. The latter were not composers in the occidental sense, however, for with few exceptions this music was handed on without having been written down: the Arabs neither adopted nor developed antique notation. On the other hand they did translate, comment on, and extend antique musical theory within the frame of their philosophy, which began its efflorescence in the 9th century. Scholarly general historians and philosophers—Al-Kindi, Al-Farabi, Avicenna, and others— left important writings on music. Yet their theories had little effect on practice. The rational working out of concepts and notation was perfected only in the West, not in the Orient.

The Iconoclastic spirit of Islam found positive expression in ornamentation, the achievement in which this culture area excels over others. Singing accompanied the weaving of carpets in such a manner that temporal rhythm was transposed into spacial order. Eduard Hanslick later sought, inversely, to make clear the nature of absolute music through the visible patterns of the arabesque. The Arabs themselves, however, did not carry abstraction in music so far; they did not cultivate the abstract forms of instrumental music as assiduously as visual ornamentation. In general they much preferred vocal to instrumental music: Al-Farabi says that the latter is tiring in the long run and should only serve as an introduction and interludes to singing or as exercises. Moreover Turkey and other countries cultivated a sort of program music: forms that, like the Greek nomoi for the aulos, represented happenings in the external world, such as the hunt or a ball game. Al-Farabi distinguishes three kinds of music. To quote from the French translation of d'Erlanger:

> The first calls forth in us an agreeable sensation, delicious, reposeful. The second has these same qualities and, in addition, it excites our imagination, creates pictures in the soul. This music suggests ideas, expresses them so that they take form in our soul. The first acts upon our ear as a decorative design does on our eye. The role of the second kind of music is therefore comparable to that of an imitative painting . . . The third kind of music is inspired by our passions, by the state of our soul: man, and every animal endowed with voice, emits special sounds according to whether he is joyful or under the sway of suffering.

The instrumental music of this culture area is not on an equal footing with its world-famous ornamentation, yet flowery melody with many ornamental notes, trills, and mannerisms is certainly one of its outstanding characteristics. A vibrating voice and curlycue line are preferred to pearly tones and plastic form. The voice avoids large intervals and moves in a small range with many nuances in timbre and tone-production. The Arabs have developed the old prose rhythms and go in for complicated beats, especially in drum playing. As a rule they stick to heptatonic scales corresponding to the Greek and medieval modes, but differentiated in a variety of tonalities. The foundation is diatonic; the constant use of microtones was rare in practice, at least before the 17th century. Characteristic is the frequency of the augmented second.

Unlike Western style, the Islamic is extensive neither in musical time nor in musical space. Its polyphony is limited, apart from the use of polyrhythms, to simultaneous variants of the melody (heterophony), to bourdon that occurs particularly in preludes, and to occasional chords that ornament or reinforce. Its forms, of which the chief types are suite, rondo, and a series of contrasting pieces in rhythms strict or free, amount not so much to architectonic structures in time as to endless spinnings out. Often the melodic movement enters suddenly, ends abruptly. It is not so much centrifugal as inclined to cling close to the fundamental tone but without accentuating or exploiting it. For all its nervous restlessness this sensitive art is shaped by the way of life underlying the idea of kismet and the persistently mobile arabesque.

Despite certain preliminary studies its influence on Western music has not yet been comprehensively looked into. For a long time it was superimposed on the music of southern Europe and a mutual cooperation in musical activities went on at least into the 15th century, when, for example, Oswald von Wolkenstein (1377–1445), one of the last Minnesingers, took part in a "song contest." Several instruments have come down to us from this culture, such as the short-necked lute, the name of which also comes from the Arabic "al'ud." In the writings of certain theoreticians we encounter Arabic technical terms. And certain forms and style elements in chivalric monophony and in the 14th century may also be explained in the light of such Arabic influences. One should remember that in the early Middle Ages the Arabs enjoyed a superior level of culture. In more recent times, of course, the West came to surpass in dynamism and expansion this historic partner against whom it did battle, first in France and Spain, then during the Crusades, and later in the Turkish wars.

 III

THE THIRD AGE

THE SPECIAL POSITION OF WESTERN MUSIC

Not to exceed the limits planned for the present volume, I shall deal but briefly with this chapter on Western music. Brevity is justified by the fact that by far the largest part of writings on music history concern themselves only with this field, and there are many works available that deal comprehensively with it. Musicology and the public have a much better view of this period than of the other three Ages. I shall therefore restrict myself to an appreciation of the special position of Western musical art among cultures and its importance in the preparation of the Fourth, our present Age. The other three chapters naturally also contain some contributions on the subject.

Western musical art is not an aggregate of all music in Europe from prehistoric times to the present, but a historical complex of trends and traditions that began in Carolingian times and projects into our own age. Developed among Romanic and Germanic peoples, it has spread in modern times over Europe and the whole world. Accordingly it is to be thought of as primarily not a geographic but a historical phenomenon. Nor does it, as Jacques Handschin says, represent a type of music culture, as though there were other representatives of the same type; it is *sui generis*. Its achievements and its fruits are unique in the history of the world; it has no counterpart. For it has not only lent expression to a family of peoples and out of folk music evolved a high art, but it has also solved unique and objective tasks important in the context of universal history, such as the full development of written composition and script-based instruction in music. For this reason, independent of the decline of "colonialism," its theory has become the basis of music theory and education in all parts of the earth, and a selection from its creations forms the foundation of the world's music literature.

 1

ESSENTIAL CHARACTERISTICS AND COURSE OF DEVELOPMENT

"Western culture" in the historical sense of the word took form when Western Europe, heretofore a part of the Roman Empire and its intercontinental commercial and cultural system, was separated from the other parts and became independent. Through the spread of Islam the Mediterranean area was split into a northern and a southern zone, and in various phases division also took place between the Western and Eastern Roman Empire, Latin and Byzantine culture, the Western and Eastern Church. Thus the northwestern part of the Old World came to depend on itself. In maintaining its independence against Huns and Arabs, in the rise of the Roman Catholic Church, and out of Charlemagne's empire the Western community developed its own culture and style, with its unique musical art. This art did of course have deep roots in ancient Western-European traditions and especially in the high cultures of the Mediterranean area, but little by little it came to be stamped with its own characteristics, which distinguished it from all other music in the world. One of its particular creations is the score, the readable note-picture in which a polyphonic work of art is graphically presented. Further, to these characteristics and special achievements belong logical harmony, wide-spanned architecture, as in fugue and symphony, intentional presentation of spiritual or emotional content in autonomous compositions.

Western musical art was impregnated as no other by scholarly and, in the broad sense, scientific theory. In mensural rhythm, in the rules governing tonality, in harmony it was rationalized through and through. The seemingly irrational world of tone was laid down *imperio rationis*—under the command of reason, as was said following Boethius—in concepts and written signs. There took shape systems of relationship and forms of presentation, like the coordinating system of the score, metrical schemes using barline and time signature, the well-tempered keyboard. More than anywhere else music was objective spirit and *scientia musica*. Musicology has rightly dealt exhaustively with the history of theory, appreciating its masters, such as Guido of Arezzo, Franco of Cologne, Jacob of Liège, Tinctoris, Zarlino, Rameau.

Rationalization, which Max Weber in particular stresses as a basic feature of Western music, did not suppress by compulsory organization what Nature provided, but revealed and emphasized those "natural orders" that rest upon simple numerical relations or pregnant fundamental forms—for example the major mode and periods of $(2 + 2) + 4$ measures and their multiples. Renewed naturalness and humanism take command, whether directly as in the Viennese classics or more vigorously stylized and superimposed in a polyphonic network as in old Netherlandish chanson-Masses and Bach's chorale arrangements. This holds for the Middle Ages also; rhythm and tonality in Perotin and other composers differ remarkably little from those of contemporaneous dance tunes. Characteristic, furthermore, is the preference for the voice singing naturally in contrast to the stylization and exotic effects widely favored in early times and in the Orient.

Western music has done for mankind something similar to what Greek sculpture, architecture, logic, and mathematics did: it strongly set forth classic fundamentals of universal character. In no other culture has songlike melody been so developed and brought to prominence, and nowhere to the same extent have architectonic forms been built out of pregnant motifs and themes. Pregnance of this sort, as in geometrical figures, no less than rationality in simple numerical relations, is one aspect of universal validity. This above all explains the diffusion of Western music today in all parts of the earth. Its "world empire" rests essentially upon its immanent universality.

But the special position of Western music is also due to the manner in which its characteristics and its basic forms have taken shape. It differs from the music of other cultures not only in its nature but also in its historical dynamic. This is often interpreted simply as springing from the "Faustian creative urge" or as the result of evolutions and revolutions in style, whereas in truth it consists at the same time and primarily in the gradual conquering of inherent and objective problems through prolonged common effort. In accord with this dynamic and with historical logic continuous developments took place, like the thorough rationalization of rhythmic notation or the perfecting and exhaustive working out of modulation among the 24 tonalities of the major-minor system. Such developmental features form the framework of Western music history, while changing styles of different periods, like Baroque and Romantic, and the manifold national styles fill in the picture with characteristic colors. The historical significance of masters like Josquin, Monteverdi, Bach, or Haydn consisted not only in their having given expression to their own character and that of their time and country in great works, but in their having mastered the objective tasks set them by the state of development at which music had arrived in their times. They did not always, indeed, serve a supposed progress towards the ever better; but without any doctrinaire ideas of progress they actually and objectively labored at the shaping of genres like fugue and sonata and at solving problems of form, like imitative counterpoint and thematic development, and in this way they consistently carried further what their predecessors had attained. Like research men concerned with the solution of scientific problems, composers, theoreticians, and practical musicians went after problems that arose from their material itself, consistently

COMPARISON OF THE
FOUR AGES IN PICTURES

To illustrate the differences and the connections between the Four Ages of Music the plates have been arranged in the following groups:

1 and 2 Magic influence of music on man and beast: The Apollo myth passed into the Christian belief (1). Shamanistic traditions (2b) rooted in the rites of pretotemic sorcerer-priests of the early Stone Age (2a). The charismatic magic-working musician lives on in figures like the demonic *Red Fiddler* (2c).

3 Sound-producing media in the Four Ages: In primitive times, natural objects like bones (a), later clay utensils (b); in the high cultures of Antiquity and the Orient a multiplicity of specifically musical, often costly melody instruments (c); since the Third Age polyphonic keyboard instruments (3d, 8c); in the Technical Age discs (8d, 9c) and radically artificial generation of sound (3e).

4 and 5 Body movement and notation: Procession or dance with instruments (4a); playing while seated, tones marked by arm or hand (5a); development of notation and script culture (5b, 6c, 4b, 8d).

6 Music and religion: Singing gives strength (mana), wards off evil, reconciles the spirits of Nature (a; cf. also 2a); from primitive tribe to the Christian congregation of global civilization (a and b); religious music as work of art in the Third Age (c). Cf. also music and divinity in Antiquity (3c).

7 Music in meditation and in education: Far Eastern contemplativeness; Hellenistic *Paideia; ars musica* in the Middle Ages.

8 Music as a sphere of genteel manners in highly cultivated modes of living (b and c; cf. also 3c and 7b) between primitive times (a; cf. also 2a) and the present (d; cf. also 9b and c).

9 The anonymous audience in the modern Age. In contrast cf. the intimate court concert (8b and c), art music in the liturgy (6c), the esoteric performance with audience present (8d).

1 "Magic" and "charm" of music. David with his harp, on the model of Orpheus. Byzantine miniature, from the Paris Psalter (middle 10th century)

2a Upper Stone Age "sorcerer" with musical bow. Trois Frères cave (Ariège)

2b Shaman of Kamchatka. In their cult a drum replaced the bow

2c Lyonel Feininger, *The Red Fiddler*, 1934

3a Natural objects for generating sound in primitive times.
a. Bone flute, early Stone Age; b. Clay drum, later Stone Age

3c Classical instruments of high cultures of Antiquity. Apollo
and Muses with lyre, harp, aulos

3d Keyboard instrument of Western polyphony. Organ in the cathedral at Constance

3e Electronic generation of sound, in the Technical Age. Control desk in studio at Cologne

4a Procession of Assyrian musicians

4b Spiritualized script culture of the West. Max Oppenheimer,
The String Quartet, 1916

5a   Music and dance on an old Egyptian tomb with hand signs
of the singers

5b   Singing from notation in Ancient Greece. Two boys with
music rolls, a youth with lyre

6a   Song at bush-clearing in the West African jungle

6b   Singing spirituals

6c Polyphonic art music in the liturgy. 15th-century choir
under the composer Ockeghem

7a Chinese poet with zither. 3rd century A. D.

7b Musical instruction in classical Athens

7c *Ars musica*, 13th century (Bibl. Ste. Geneviève, Paris)

8a Women with musical bows. Rock painting, South-West Africa

8b Female musicians at the Chinese court

8c Baroque court music. C. van Loo, *The Concert*

8d Recording of works by Anton Webern on discs, Robert
Craft conducting

9a   Furtwängler conducting the Berlin Philharmonic

9b

"A Handel concert in the village" (title page of an issue of the East Berlin periodical *Music und Gesellschaft*

9c At a record shop

SOURCES OF THE ILLUSTRATIONS

1   Miniature from the Paris Psalter (10th century). Reproduced in John Beckwith, *The Art of Constantinople*, Phaidon Press Ltd., 1961 (distributed by New York Graphic Society, Greenwich, Conn.), Plate 84, p. 70.

2a   Herbert Kühn, *Die Felsbilder Europas*, 1952.

2b   J. G. Georgi, *Beschreibung aller Nationen des Russischen Reiches*, 1776; *Fischer-Lexikon Völkerkunde*, ed. H. Tischner, p. 159.

2c   Hans Hess, *Lyonel Feininger*, 1958, Plate 18.

3a   Otto Seewald, *Beiträge zur Kenntnis der steinzeitlichen Musikinstrumente Europas*, 1934, Plate II, No. 1.

3b   Landesmuseum für Vorgeschichte, Forschungsstelle für die Bezirke Halle und Magdeburg.

3c   Friedrich Behn, *Musikleben im Altertum und frühen Mittelalter*, 1954, Plate 54.

3d   Photo by Helga Schmidt-Glassner, Stuttgart.

3e   MGG, III, col. 1265/66, photo by Dr. Herbert Eimert, Westdeutscher Rundfunk.

4a   British Museum, London.

4b   Oesterreichische Galerie, Vienna.

5a   Jacques Handschin, *Musikgeschichte im Überblick*, 1948, Plate II.

5b   Staatl. Museum, Berlin, 2549 F, Egert Pöhlmann, *Griech. Musikfragmente*, 1960, frontispiece.

6a   H. and U. Himmelheber, *Die Dan*, 1958, Ill. 1a.

6b   Press Section of the American Embassy in Bad Godesberg.

6c   Bibliothèque Nationale, Paris, Ms. Franc. 1537, fol. 58v.

7a   Illustrated edition of *Lieh-hsien-chuan*, Ming Period, MGG, II, Plate 40/3.

7b   Friedrich Behn, *Musikleben im Altertum und frühen Mittelalter*, 1954, Plate 52.

7c   Bibliothèque Ste. Geneviève, Paris, Ms. 1273, fol. 98v.

8a   *Der Mensch der Urzeit*, ed. A. Varagnac, 1960, Plate 13.

8b   British Museum, London.

8c   Max Sauerlandt, *Die Musik in fünf Jahrhunderten der europäischen Malerei*, 1922, p. 148.

8d   Columbia Records.

9a   Hans Engel, *Musik und Gesellschaft*, 1960, facing p. 65.

9b   Periodical *Musik und Gesellschaft*, April 1959, title page.

9c   *Propyläen Weltgeschichte*, X, 1961, p. 540.

unfolding whatever possibilities its varied content offered.

To understand the course of Western music, therefore, it is not enough to follow its changes of style; more important is the study of its developmental traits or trends. "Development" is not to be understood in its biological meaning or always in an upward sense; the objective and the result of such a trend or trait do not need to be on a higher level than earlier phases; just as the gradual simplification of a language, say English or Bulgarian, does not signify an upward development to a higher level. And furthermore developmental trends do not always proceed in a straight line; sometimes they result from a tangle of changes of which they indicate the basic direction.

Alongside the new, the old continued to survive, whether pushed aside or incorporated with it. Thus, during the advance of notated polyphony, monophony lived on in folk and liturgical song, acquiring new values in the unison and the solo sonata for a single melodic instrument. Similarly in church music, even after 1600 the cantus-firmus movement was cultivated alongside free composition without prescribed melody. So too in the 19th century diatonicism and triadic sequences were contrasted with progressive chromaticism and the use of dissonance—notably by Richard Wagner. Complete elimination of the hitherto existing never occurred before the radical directions taken by the 20th century.

Developmental trends and other historical processes have led by main roads and bypaths to definitive end forms. It is onesided to look upon all these as stagnation, as dead-end streets. In this way the multifarious notations debouched in the clearly readable score of today, the numerous rhythms, tonalities, and forms of folksong in such stereotyped schemes as strophic song-form in major mode and even measure. Classical end forms, which indeed admitted of a considerable afterlife, are for example the Palestrina style and the Bach fugue.

The self-unfolding of Western music went on for a very long time without any essential influences from outside. Only internally did it constantly absorb fructifying elements in that it drew certain melodies and general types from its own underlying strata:

from folksong, from the traditions of minstrel and fiddler, and from other areas of musical practice. The history of polyphony in the Middle Ages is not, as Friedrich Ludwig assumes, to be taken as a wholly intrinsic development in which one step followed from another, the new element in the accompanying voice being at first only its range, then its own melodic movement, later its own rhythm, lastly its own text. Rather, various kinds of unwritten polyphony were both simultaneously and successively taken up in written composition and so given artistic form, these processes working together with features that were properly speaking developmental.

FULL GRAPHIC NOTATION AND THE
MUSICAL WORK OF ART

All high cultures are script cultures, but only the Western fully evolved the written presentation of music and developed it into a general basis of musical practice and education. This development had the following aspects:

1. At first practically only liturgical songs were notated, then others also and finally all genres. Almost without exception instrumentalists played without notes during the whole Middle Ages. During modern times and especially in the 19th century, both folksong and entertainment music were also notated, although favorite tunes had of course already been written down in contrafacta and arrangements for several voices.

2. The spread of music was much facilitated by printing, which came into use for Gregorian melodies in 1476 and after 1501 for the publication of polyphonic works. Printing meant an im-

portant step in the diffusion of musical compositions among the people, in other countries and parts of the world, and into the future. Through it the capacity of music to survive was markedly strengthened and the way prepared for the building of a world literature of music.

3. While in ancient Greece theory and notation stood far apart, in the Middle Ages theory had a decisive influence on the development of notation. Even its early treatises, contrary to any of Antiquity, contain examples in notation—for instance, the *Musica enchiriadis*.

4. At first only pitches were notated, rhythm but partially. In the course of the Middle Ages rhythm, and to some extent tempo also, came to be more precisely represented in mensural notation, and in modern times the secondary elements—dynamics, agogics, instrumentation—as well as emotional character and manner of performance have been more and more expressly prescribed. Thus the development was moving towards the goal of objectively specifying all the elements of music (cf. music exx. 20–22).

5. The staffless neumes assisted the memory and complemented oral tradition. Later forms of notation also reckoned with "the loss of things taken for granted." The purpose of the development, however, was to make notation as far as possible independent of tradition, and accordingly to give the clearest possible indication of what the composer meant.

6. Western notation tends towards a graphic note-picture, a design to strike the eye. It is a "drawing" of the composition with its ups and downs in melody and its higher and lower voices in counterpoint. Thus it is visible and abstract at the same time: "visible abstraction," like a map. Supplanting the less obvious letter and number notations, this legible note-picture took over completely in modern times.

7. While the primary purpose of letter notation was in the main to indicate the position of the fingers on the instrument— that is to say, the execution—linear notation primarily represents the music to be performed. Thus its development to sole supremacy also indicates the trend towards representing the composition itself, the work of art objectified.

8. Out of the endeavor to demonstrate visually the composition itself, by the late 16th century the score was achieved, the graphic simultaneous presentation of all voices in one field of vision.

9. The development tended towards indication of all the elements involved as well as towards simplicity and general comprehensibility. In the 17th and 18th centuries it led to a final stage beyond which only little has been changed or added.

10. Only when exact transcription of both extra-European music and complex European folk music became necessary did Western notation in our own century add further signs. Such writing down of music already being played and heard is different in character from our traditional notation: it is not *pre*scription but *tran*scription; it shows not so-it-should-be-done but so-it-is.

Western culture produced the completely notated musical work of art and created a formal theory of composition. Before that, music, like the dance, had existed primarily as improvisation along certain guidelines. Now, however, it acquired a mode of existence like works of literature and for the theater. That the composer little by little came to prescribe all the elements of music means also that these became constituent parts of composition. Thus the figured bass, which the cembalist had to fill in according to his taste and capacity, was replaced by the *accompagnamento obbligato*, while the composer also undertook to fix ornamentation and virtuoso cadenzas himself. The practical musician lost his creative share almost wholly to the composer and became an interpreter. With this was established the norm of adhering exactly to the note-picture and rendering unaltered what was there prescribed.

Until the 16th century the share of the composer and of what he had prescribed had been limited to the setting down of pitch, rhythm, and polyphony. But then, and especially after 1600, it expanded to take in the whole sonorous foreground and also the psycho-spiritual background of the music. The composer now determined the sound-volume by dynamic marks, at first contrasting whole sections in *forte* and *piano*, and since the mid-18th century graduating the dynamics more and more, from *ppp* to *fff*, indicating not only abrupt transitions but gradual swelling and lessening, crescendo and diminuendo, and in the "vermanirierten Mannheimer goût" (the mannered taste of the Mannheim school, with which Leopold Mozart reproached his son) letting various dynamic degrees succeed each other at closest range. Likewise he now specified tempo and agogics and also the instruments to be used. The nature of the composition changed. Instead of a neutral setting, not conceived for particular instruments and often even leaving open a choice between instrumental and vocal performance, it now became the fully specified opus in which timbre was just as much composed as the tonal structure. Accordingly instrumental and vocal style, ensemble and orchestral style, ways of composing for piano, organ, violin, flute, all became much more differentiated than before. So also there arose for every instrumental setting a repertory of its own, whereas previously instrumental music had consisted largely of "intabulations," transcriptions of vocal works and one and the same piece was intended to be sung or played, for organ or for other keyboard instruments.

A fully notated work can be better built than music scriptlessly transmitted. Western culture was the first to give architectonic form to long spans of time by purely musical means. Highly artistic forms, like fugue and sonata, are among the most characteristic contributions it brought forth in comparison with all other cultures. Only in modern times did this feature fully develop. The older contrapuntal forms—the canon, for example— are for the most part to be regarded as types of setting rather than as determining, like sonata form, the relation of the successive sections and so the course of the whole. Even the polyphonic Mass, which arose in the 14th century as a cyclical work and in the middle of the 15th became unified through having the same cantus firmus in all movements, was at that time not yet so fully organized by specifically musical means as the symphony. In forms of the modern era, principally those of absolute music, all purely musical elements were exploited for the building of purely musical structures: sequence of tonalities and modulations, especially in fugue and sonata; differences of tempo (e.g. fast-slow-fast), volume and instrumentation, as for example, alternation of tutti and solo or minuet and trio; types of composition like overture and rondo-finale; symmetry, return and contrast, as in the three- or four-movement cycle of the sonata.

Like the sonorous foreground, the inherent and transmusical content of a composition was shaped comparatively late by the composer himself. In this the history of music differs from those of literature and the plastic arts. The leading ideas of Gothic, Mystic, Scholastic times found no such rich expression in musical monuments as did those of Goethe's time and the Romantics. The influence of Josquin des Prez was epoch-making: he differed from earlier masters not nearly so much in his more subjective and individual style as in that he expressed in the musical fabric of written composition important general ideas, notably the essence of Christian faith and prayer. Everywhere in the world music was concerned with primal phenomena like love, ethos, the sacred; but what once had been left to effects upon the hearer, to participation in supramusical contexts, to empathy and imaginative interpretation of symbols, composers since Josquin have impressed objectively into their works. They so shaped the musical substance of composition that such content became transparent. All cultures linked music and religion, but it was Western culture that first fully unfolded musical works of religious content. By pictorial effects and tonal language it expressly set forth such content, as Bach did, for example, in his Passions.

Adrian Petit Coclico praised Josquin and other composers who knew how to express "all affects" in their works. The word "affect" has today become stale and empty and does not adequately express the concepts or emotions here represented in tone and timbre. They are not only affects but whole idea-areas, like the union of majesty and fascination, the august and the miraculous that we call the sacred, or the idea of eternal life and blessedness, or the complex of sweetness-and-light, purity and grace concentrated in the figure of the Virgin Mary. Later, idea-areas in which the sensible is interwoven with the visible and intellectual were often characterized by a word—for example, "Eroica" or "Pastorale." These idea-areas have flourished and faded in the course of history, so that an outsider may think he is hearing only "sounding forms," whereas to those who are familiar with the style and language or as historians feel their way into the contemporaneous situation, sound and form reveal content and open vistas.

The same applies to those types of absolute instrumental music that go back to types of vocal or use-music, taking over as an aura something of the atmosphere and content these pieces stood for—ballades of Chopin and Brahms, for example, the berceuse, barcarole, serenade, and so forth. The transformation of dance-pieces into the art-form of the suite, and similar processes, show the modern development of music into a self-reliant art. Leaving behind its manifold connections with life and its position as a scholarly discipline among the liberal arts, music entered the circle of the fine arts and was now considered an esthetically autonomous world in itself. This transformation took place in all types of composition. Thus the oratorios of Handel or Beethoven's *Missa solemnis* stand on their own feet as works of art even though they remain linked with the traditions of church music. Despite these bonds and despite all continuance and all revival of life-linked types, the ever-growing self-reliance of the art of music was a basic feature of its evolution. In the measure that it ceased to be part and function of extraneous activities—worship, or court, or festival—an independent musical life sprang up, with its own institutions and concert halls, its audiences, its music literature, its own esthetic, and so on. The forms of an autonomous culture area took shape, familiar to us but alien to all earlier cultures. Music became a "splendid, autocratic art," as Herder called it, who, on the other hand also paid tribute to its significance as *Hausmusik* and as the voice of humanity and of the nations.

THE WEALTH OF STYLES AND WORKS

That the main and basic store of the world's musical literature is constituted by a selection of Western works acquires still greater weight because of the variety of styles it includes. So far as style consists in the coining of characteristic individuality, not every group and person has a style of their own, their own note; instead, out of a quantity of colorless music there arise, as strong personalities arise out of the mass, composers and communities distinguished by certain stylistic elements or by a style of their own.

In music history the West has, if not always, at least particularly often, offered good conditions for the unfolding of distinctive personalities and personal styles. Haydn throws light on the circumstances that favored such individuality when he says: "As leader of an orchestra I was able to experiment, to observe what brings out an impression, and what weakens it, and so to improve, add, cut out, dare; I was separated from the world. Nobody around me could confuse and bother me about myself, and so I had to become original." The statement holds for the other outstanding ardent spirits and personalities, original geniuses among the masters. They experimented, but in the sense of actually experiencing how new ideas might be concretely realized; through their experience as conductors, concertizing pianists, or men of the theater, they arrived at new ideas. They were nonconformist enough to take their task hard and not to rest self-satisfied in the beaten track, but not so nonconformist as those eccentrics who avoid encounters with reality. They dedicated themselves to their special world without becoming isolated and faced their environment with its concrete realities without falling victim to it.

Haydn combined practical demands of his art with friendliness to others in a humanistic manner and could join in with the contemporary concept of the original genius, though his whole nature ran counter to the storm-and-stress current of his time. Yet the same fundamental ideas he thus stands for have been lived and voiced in every century of the West's modern era, albeit with variations and with various motives. Luther himself pointed out the nature of genius in the works of Josquin des Prez, explaining it by the opposition between law and grace. Where only law commands, work and its results are sour and joyless; where mercy, *gratia, charisma*, are active however, work goes along very well. So God preaches the good news through music also: in Josquin the superiority of grace and mercy becomes evident; his compositions flow forth gaily and gently, not driven or constrained by rules.

Since the 15th century the leading composers tower so high out of the whole musical life of their time that the history of Western music might be presented simply through its creative masters. But this would be a onesided view; quite as important as individual personalities are also the peoples, the classes of society, and the currents of the time. Since the Middle Ages the Western nations had been combining international with national features in their characteristic modifications of forms common to all. If, for example, one compares the tune of the later Hildebrand song [1] with a French version of the same type, a melody to the historical song *Reveillez-vous, Piccars!*, characteristic differences appear between the two national styles. French singing combines a pungent clarity with charm and élan, likes precise accents and sharply punctuated rhythms. The German version is more restless and impulsive; the melodic movement here has more drive and flow, it lingers and darts ahead, and is more mimetically expressive. Similar characteristic differences in style exist among different versions of the same melodic formulas as used by northern French trouvères, Provençal troubadours, German minnesingers,

---

[1] A melody handed down since the 16th century but probably originating in the 13th at the latest. Cf. the author's *Sammlung europäischer Volksgesang* (Cologne 1952), p. 64 ff.

and in Italian laude and Spanish cantigas.

National styles became still richer and more pronounced from the 15th century on and more mutually fructifying, as witness the contrasts between madrigal, chanson, and German lied or between opera buffa, opéra comique and singspiel. Characteristic for this variety of national styles in the West are compositions contrasting several such styles with each other; there is, for instance, a set of variations by Alessandro Poglietti (d. 1683) in which a theme is treated in the styles of diverse races in Austria and the Empire. To be considered also are the works of great masters who took up and exploited various national styles, like Bach, Mozart, Wagner. Discussion of such differences, which was especially popular in the 18th century, tells us something about national psychologies. Mattheson says (1713) that in music the Italians are best at execution and surprise, the French at diverting and charming, the Germans at composing and studying, the English at judging and recompensing. Yet the nations' awareness of their own and their neighbors' special qualities was in general too rough and generalized to reflect the various nuances in these actual differences. Furthermore national styles were not fixed from the beginning and for all time. They developed, changed, weakened in the course of history. The history of European music is certainly not to be understood as a juxtaposition of several almost unalterable psychic national predispositions, each of which moved into the foreground at a different time, nor as the struggle for hegemony between a race that from the outset heard horizontally and one that *a priori* heard vertically.

Peoples, social classes, cities that played a part in determining the course of Western music history and brought to maturity in their time its wealth of notable characters and colorings, arose in favorable constellations to their full historic significance and with the setting of these constellations withdrew into the background. Similarly, Christianity did not at once and everywhere infuse the music of the church and of the rest of the Christian world with its spirit, but was obliged to prevail over other historical forces and, after setbacks, to attempt renewal. The spiritual and the temporal, the sacred and the profane were never set upon the same level, as some think who misunderstand the *contrafacta* that turned secular into spiritual melodies and vice versa; they were antitheses that again and again set new problems. A lasting tension existed between them, as between Church and State, that "inner dynamic in which Western culture had the advantage over every sort of pure theocracy or purely secular state," as Eduard Spranger expresses it. Only because they were a fruitful solution of such tensions, above the extremes of purism and secularization, could the great works of Christian musical art—of Dufay and Josquin, Lassus and Schütz, Bach and Bruckner—come into being. They form a peak in the history of the West and over and above this in the history of the human spirit. In Hegel's words, "this fundamental religious music belongs to the most profound and the most influential that any art can produce."

PREPARATION OF THE FOURTH AGE

The early phase of the modern period began about 1500. It began with humanism, the Reformation, the printing of music, Josquin des Prez and other composers, the frottola and the madrigal, and so forth. The term "Renaissance," in music particularly, does not help us much in characterizing and epitomizing the historically important events of this epoch. The modern period proper, however, as in philosophy and science (Descartes, Bacon, Kepler, Galileo, Huygens, et al.) did not start till around 1600: when opera and oratorio originated and countless other types of vocal and instrumental music; when the secondary elements of music were taken into composition and the church modes were replaced by the major-minor system with its scales transposable into 24 keys, rich chromaticism and the use, soon to unfold, of dissonant chords.

In the modern period in the West almost all the evolutionary traits began that run through our own period, the first stage of the Fourth Age of music. The 19th century, especially, is at once a mighty finale to the Third Age and a prelude to the Fourth. "This century," says Hans Freyer, "is much more powerful than we even today, at the distance of more than one generation, are able to estimate. Whoever looks at it merely as a period in European history does not do it justice. The immense productivity it unchained within the limited area of the West is like a mere echo of its world-historic significance."

Soon after its beginnings Western culture started to spread to Eastern Europe, and with the start of the modern era began its expansion over the whole globe. Whatever the individual differences, in every country similar forms of adaptation and assimilation resulted. Missionaries, settlers, traveling musicians brought folk music and Gregorian chant: courts attracted virtuosos and opera troupes; islands of Western music arose in an Eastern environment. Over and above this, indigenous creative talents adopted Western forms and styles. Thus in the 17th century Western polyphony permeated Russian chant, and Russia took over the "world-dominating note-and-staff system" which with its "imposing simplicity," as Otto Riesemann points out, had no difficulty whatever in replacing the old notation of Russian chant. In the days of Catherine II composers like Dmitri Bortniansky (1751–1825) followed Western patterns in accord with the aims of Peter the Great.

With the "awakening" of the nations began the collecting of indigenous folk material, with which native composers, like Mussorgsky, were busying themselves by the 19th century. Western composers—Mendelssohn and Schumann, for example—wrote works using national color characteristics of various countries. In so doing they came to fabricate some imaginary national atmosphere, as in the make-believe Hungarian and Spanish music of Liszt, Brahms, Bizet. But above all, new national styles of their own developed in the various countries of East as well as West

Europe. This "process of nationalization" is not just to be equated with "the replacement of the universal Graeco-Roman gods by provincial divinities," as Alfred Einstein would have us believe, but also means that those European peoples who did not take part, or a central part, in the development of Western music, from now on cultivated styles of their own amalgamating Western structures with indigenous traditions. Already with Chopin and most definitely with Mussorgsky, Smetana, Dvořák, and others the forming of such styles was connected with nationalist political aspirations.

The historical importance of these movements lies not merely in their contribution to the history of nationalism in the world. Rather they indicate also a re-animation of old and archaic forms of music that were not limited to a single nation but spread over all Europe and far beyond. When for example Chopin or Grieg used both the augmented fourth and double-bourdon, in tonality and elementary polyphony they were renewing not specifically Polish or Norwegian traits but a common possession from archaic times. The so-called national schools of the 19th century began to revive extra- and pre-Western layers of music, not only expanding the Western art of composition through their use but leading it out beyond its boundaries: Debussy, Bartók, Janáček, Falla, and others continued this process, which has long since reached into other parts of the world. More will be said about this in the next chapter.

With the expansion of Western science, technique, and music throughout Europe and the globe, the modern era has cleared the way for the planetary civilization of the Fourth Age. At the same time it has prepared the present-day position of music in relation to the public and in the various levels of a post-bourgeois, democratic or socialist society. It developed the public concert and other forms of musical life of society at large without class barriers. Following the philanthropic Enlightenment many songs were composed for the people, and since Herder the characteristic traditions of urban and rural populations have been collected and brought to a second life. Herein research, popular education, and renovation have cooperated. From the viewpoint of general history the most varied events contributing to this process are elements in a historical complex: for example, the rise of the Prussian public school system with the introduction of singing as an obligatory branch of public-school instruction and teachers' seminars (1809); the upsurge in Germany of male choruses; the collecting of folksongs by Ludwig Erk, Zuccalmaglio, Erben, Kolberg, and others; the folksong settings since Silcher and Brahms; the youth movement in Germany at the turn of the 19th century, the simultaneous folksong movement in Austria around Josef Pommer, and similar movements in other countries.

In a series of renascences the modern era developed the Western world's consciousness of history and set in motion the collecting of all mankind's musical heritage. First came the turning back to Antiquity in humanism and to old church music, to Gregorian chant and polyphony from Palestrina to Bach. Here too research, revival of old works, and renewing of old styles lent each other wings. The awareness and study of music history expanded and took command in research and education. On the model of the humanistic revival of antique culture each of these renascences unfolded a historical pattern in which an earlier period was transfigured, the intervening time appeared as a decline, and to the present fell the task of bending the curve of history's course upward again to prepare for a new flowering.

In such views of the world and of music, thinking revolved around history and the future and this links these renascence movements with progressive tendencies like those surrounding Wagner and Liszt. 1830 was the year that saw the revival of Bach's *St. Matthew Passion* but also the first performance of Berlioz's *Symphonie fantastique*. In 1850 the Bachgesellschaft was formed and Wagner's *Das Kunstwerk der Zukunft* (*The Art-work of the Future*) appeared. The coincidence of such dates indicates not only contrast, for the progressive parties of the 19th century strove, unlike the avant-gardism of today, both for the new and for renewal, widely re-incorporating old style-elements. Innately characteristic for Wagner is not only his advancing the development of chromaticism, dissonant chord construction, declamatory rhythm, and so forth, but also his drawing upon the revived heritage from Bach and Palestrina, Gregorian chant and archaic monophony, and playing up the contrast between old and new conceptions in works like *Parsifal* with its distinction between the realm of the Knights of the Grail and Klingsor's enchanted garden.

The rapid evolution of chromaticism, dissonance, modulation, etc. was made possible through broadening or else discarding the old conception of the harmonic significance of music. Heretofore music counted primarily as the paradigm of beautiful, blissful "harmonious" agreement. It was held to reflect the eternal harmony of the macrocosm and to be a means of expressing and bringing to effect the inner harmony of the microcosm, the health and happiness of mankind, *musica humana.* This view continued well into the modern era; it was upheld as an example by Ronsard, for instance, and likewise by Shakespeare in *The Merchant of Venice,* newly substantiated by Kepler, Werckmeister, Bach, and, following this tradition, glorified in poetry by Goethe. Visible models for the nature and effect of music were the figures of Orpheus taming the wild element in animal and man with harmony, or of David healing the sick and melancholy king with his harp playing. Not until the 19th century did it become customary to represent rather than combat wildness and sickness through music. It had lain in neither the intent nor the capacity of music in the Middle Ages to depict the Inferno as Dante did. Now, however, Weber, Meyerbeer, Berlioz, Wagner, and others found in such materials and figures—the wolf's den, the witches' Sabbath, Ortrud, Kundry—the richest possibilities for further development of dissonance, enhanced chromaticism, harsh and uncanny sounds. The question was discussed whether the scene in the wolf's den over-stepped musical limits and whether the devil was not too unmusical to be represented in music. But the development went further; it led to representation of the perverse and the horrible, as in Strauss's *Salome* and *Elektra,* and further to the opposition on principle against music as the symbol of harmony. It is indicative of the disharmonization of music that the sharpest dissonances now became elements in "harmonic theory."

If one looks upon the 19th century *not* from the standpoint of those movements that were striving away from it, it seems like a splendid flowering or at least a luminously multicolored autumn of music's Third Age. Works of Chopin, Berlioz, Liszt, Wagner, Verdi, Richard Strauss far surpass the music of earlier times in color, differentiation of hues, expressive nuance. Over-rich in tone-colors and chord-formations, chromatics and modulations, dynamic shading and variety of expression, works like Strauss's *Don Juan* or *Salome* appear to be peaks and endpoints of a development.

At the same time, however, signs of stagnation and atrophy gave indication of a process that, often interpreted as decadence, was just as much transition to the Fourth Age as decline of the Third. The possibility of finding new chords and modulations within the framework of the major-minor system came to an end. Rapid passage into remote tonalities had become easy and smooth, losing its value as it lost the character of genuine modulation. Similarly, the exploitation of always further dynamic possibilities, begun around 1600, was practically closed off with Max Reger and his contemporaries. In addition came the decline of old folk-traditions, a decline consisting not only in their "dying out" but also in their loss of fecundity and the simplification into stereotyped major (cf. music ex. 42). Even in the church congregational singing lived almost entirely off its heritage from earlier times, and after the 19th century occidental culture in Europe no longer wrote its own dance music but subsisted on importations from North and South America. And together with all this, art music lost those sources from which it had drawn since the beginning of Western culture; this material too had been used up.

Yet this does not signify a "decline of the West." For in the first place the heritage of Western music is bound to remain of enduring significance. Jacob Burckhardt, it is true, said in his *Weltgeschichtliche Betrachtungen* (*Observations on World History*) that "its imperishableness" depends on "the continuation of our tonal system and rhythm, which is not eternal. Mozart and Beethoven can become as incomprehensible to a future mankind as Greek music, so highly prized by its contemporaries, is to us now. They will then remain great on credit, through the enthusiastic statements of our time, somewhat like the ancient painters whose works are no longer extant." But merely in view of the fact that in every continent Western works form the basis of musical repertory and Western theory the foundation of musical education, this assumption can probably not be sustained. In addition, comparative and methodical proofs have shown that its spread throughout the world rests upon the immanent universality of Western music and its systems.

In the second place, the fate of the West as a part of the earth is to be distinguished from the fate of Western culture as a temporally limited cultural movement. In recent years the new Europe, in music as in other fields, has shown through its achievement and vitality that it is not in the grip of a decline. There are many indications that, despite the loss of political power, even in the age of technical civilization now begun, it can and will remain musically significant.

 IV

THE FOURTH AGE

THE AGE OF TECHNIQUE AND OF GLOBAL INDUSTRIAL CULTURE

THE BEGINNING OF A NEW EPOCH

Although the determining trends of the 20th century in the main consider themselves revolutionary and expressly turn away from the period of Beethoven and Wagner, they are still in many respects continuing that period; they have inherited themes and counterpoints from a polyphonic score of many voices and they are carrying them further, whether using them as they are, or varying them, or developing them. Thus the neo-Romantic youth movement, the Schütz renaissance, and related tendencies were fresh waves in the currents that had begun with the enthusiasm for folksong inspired by Herder and with the Palestrina revival. The reaction against Romanticism, on the other hand, was linked to those more recent historical trends in opposition to which Romanticism had come into being: progressive enlightenment, realism, disillusionment. Public concert life, often pronounced dead, went on unfolding and with it the perfecting of interpretation. Today's musical life much more closely resembles that of the 19th century than that of the 17th or the 13th. The more radical tendencies of the "new" music too followed upon evolutions and crises in the period preceding, which, as we have seen, was not only the finale of the Third Age but also prelude to the Fourth. Thus Schoenberg went beyond certain elements in the *Tristan* style and freed them from the diatonic counterweights that in Wagner provide contrast and help the play of equilibrium.

It is not to be denied, however, that music is in fact taking part in a revolutionary change, and this turn in the times goes far too deep to be understood simply as reaction against the 19th century. It is leading not merely to a further period within the West, comparable to the changes around 1600 and 1750, but out over the frontiers of Europe to a new Age. This epochal change, emerging as it did in the French Revolution and with the beginnings of machine techniques, and thrusting rapidly ahead with the two world wars, is "a caesura of the first order in world history," as Alfred Weber, Karl Jaspers, Hans Freyer have shown. That with it "a new epoch of human history" began is no illusion arising from a time-bound perspective.

But if the new epoch has just begun, if its fabric is just in work, and we ourselves working along at Goethe's "whizzing loom of time," is it already possible to judge it objectively? Can we pronounce any lastingly valid views upon a time that is not yet finished and from which we stand at no distance? Only the event will tell, yet certain points we can be clear about. The greater amount of facts to be experienced and the lively immediacy of the experiencing itself are advantages for present-day knowledge that are lacking in our observation of earlier, and especially of distant, centuries. Science furthermore owes it to itself and its surrounding world not to leave the field to partisan ideologies in politics and art. Hans Freyer—in his *Theorie des gegenwärtigen Zeitalters* (*Theory of the Present Time*, 1955) and the volume of *Propyläen Weltgeschichte* entitled *Die Welt von Heute* (*The World of Today*, 1961)—has characterized the nature of ideology and the necessity for scientific analysis of one's own time. "Misty layers of traditional values and customary nomenclatures, of cliché opinions and even of misleading interpretations lie thick over present-day reality. At bottom, no one sees it as it is, but everyone sees it as 'one' sees it." To anyone who knows well enough how humanity passes from darkness to light the present is no theme for objective research but a passing stage on the road to a finer future. "If to this be added the thought that just now history is bound to go through the deepest depths of dehumanization and estrangement from all that is, before it can dialectically hasten upward to its salvation, then the present epoch achieves a value, certainly, but a perverse value, after the formula of 'the worse, the better.' "

The history of the new movement in music will no longer "tolerate any meaningful juxtaposition of opposites," says T. W. Adorno. The representatives of even serial and serial-electronic music see this music not as a trend among others but as the only trend corresponding to the present stage of composition and the state of society in process or to be expected; after the "finish of yesterday's New Music" it will be the only music that counts. This narrowing down, however, does not fit with the extraordinary multiplicity of musical tastes, which Erich Doflein has called the outstanding mark of the present. A glance at radio programs shows that the most heterogeneous sorts of old and oldest, foreign and most foreign, new and newest music are living side by side. Disparate styles and points of view jostle one another in the free world, East and West contending, and even developments in Asia and Africa belong to the present and the future of music.

Yet a pluralism that presents multiplicity merely as such still offers no picture of the time. To depict the quantity of isms, explaining it as due to specific and rapidly changing artistic intentions, still does not represent the current of history. The common assumption that there is development and progress in technique, indeed, but not in art, hinders our understanding of essential coherences in our own time. "Just now history really is proceeding in large part as progress," says Freyer, progress in the "value-free sense in which a chain reaction is sheer progress." If modern science points out developmental traits or trends in the web of history, it is not simply following the evolutionism of Rowbotham or Robert Lach, and it is equally far removed from that confident faith in progress which Richard Strauss, for one, celebrated when he praised the "glorious thought of working energetically on at the steady development of our art . . . conceiving and bringing forth something ever higher and more perfect."

Analysis of our time cannot fail to heed the fact that in music, too, far-reaching courses of development are under way. They run side by side and together, put themselves through against resistances, call forth adjustments and counter-movements. In the process they become modified, making losses as well as gains. Artistic creativity does not spend itself exclusively, it is true, in contributing to developmental trends, to be recognized by contemporaries, critics, and historians for so doing. But it is conditioned by processes like progressive technicalization and industrialization and reacts in response to them, whether in an unproductive manner or creatively.

The Europeanization of the globe, which began almost five centuries ago with the discovery and settlement of America, has led to mankind forming no longer a co-existing group of separate cultures but instead a richly intense concatenation of world trade, world politics, world civilization. The dynamic drive of Western culture, however, and the global industrial civilization that has grown out of it are working simultaneously in other dimensions; the world we know and in which we function is expanding not only in space but also in social, temporal, and organizational directions.

These expansions had already begun in part in the 19th century, in part earlier, and today they are continuing into the future. Their objective aim is universal: to span inclusion of all humanity, all peoples, all historical legacies, the sum total of possibilities. The currents that are working together at this colossal collective undertaking have mostly more limited aims; their slogans run: Spread of Christianity! International Understanding and Development Assistance! Art for the People! Collect Folksongs! Cultivate Old Music! Back to Bach, to Schütz, to Gregorian Chant! Create the New and again New! By a "trick of reason," to quote Hegel, each one of these trends serves not only its own purposes but at the same time, whether it wills or no, the universal development.

Through all these many currents the river of history is naturally split into delta form. Added to this, each expansion must assert itself against opposition, in turn provoking counter-movements.

To pursue each of these is not possible in the following analysis; from the tangle of streams we can pick out only the main water-courses.

THE SPREAD OF WESTERN MUSIC OVER
THE GLOBE AND THE BUILDING OF
A UNIVERSAL MUSICAL CULTURE

Rooted in South and West Europe, the music of Western civilization spread gradually over the whole earth: first over all Europe to its borders, again with colonization over the Americas and such parts of the remaining continents as were settled by Europeans, and thirdly among the native populations of those continents, both peoples theretofore primitive and peoples of the middle and high cultures from the Near to the Far East. In the course of this diffusion processes familiar to us from the musical history of East Europe took place in other parts of the earth. The music of Western composers was introduced; it adapted itself to the new environment; indigenous composers began to follow Western models, and finally national trends arose that combined adopted with native features. Part of the universal significance of the "national schools" of East Europe lies in their having created models for the nations of Asia and Africa striving towards a national expression of their own. In any case, this particularly favorable historical constellation will not be repeated, and where the model is but a recipe there are no creative deeds.

In the "New World" a sung Mass was celebrated by 1494 and by the 16th century church music was being composed. Settlers brought folksongs with them and in remote regions, like the

Appalachian Moutains of the United States, much has been preserved that was dying out in Europe. Churches and cities took over the changing periodic styles of Europe and in certain forms developed types of their own, as, for example, in the Latin-American church music of the 18th century or the North American singing-school movement. As a consequence of political separation from Europe, songs arose that gave expression to national sentiment, to be followed later by the "national schools" of composition in Latin America as well as the beginnings of characteristic styles in North America.

For some decades now a steep and rapid rise has been taking place. The New World has lifted itself out of the preparatory phase of colonial musical life to a level equal with today's Europe, and other countries also, like South Africa, Australia, New Zealand, are building up through concerts, radio, education, and so forth a complete musical culture on modern lines. In the United States this development was furthered by the country's rise to political and economic world power. An astonishingly large number of orchestras and other cultural institutions have sprung up there, some of which belong to the best in the world, and in a number of areas in musical life the country has become a leader. From their own internal evolution and the fusion of European, Indian, and Negro characteristics various styles have been formed in both North and South America. Certain types have achieved worldwide dissemination: South American dances, New Orleans-born jazz, and in more industrial areas the "musical" and Hollywood's film music. Many native composers have brought the new impulses to fruition and given expression in musical composition also to the self-unfolding of their countries—in the United States men like Charles Ives, an original genius and lonely forerunner of "new music," and like Roy Harris, William Schuman, Aaron Copland, like George Gershwin, to name but a few, and in Brazil, for example, Heitor Villa-Lobos.

It is customary to contrast "Western music"—the music of Europe and the Americas—with that of primitive and oriental cultures. This division of the world, however, corresponds only in part to the new reality. For these other cultures also have been and are being inundated by Western music; they are widely giving up their previous styles and forms and undergoing fundamental changes. A universal musical culture is spreading out which in many respects is no longer geographically limited. Hence this contrast holds only for a period that is already passing. In the new Age it is being covered over by relationships that reach around the whole globe.

Many forces have been at work introducing Western music into foreign cultures or are in the course of so doing: missions, schools, trade, radio, film (and sometimes television), America Houses, private foundations, development aid. The record shows how from the 16th century on missionaries have used music, and especially singing, in the conversion of natives. Today Sovietization is taking a principal part in this process: it is carrying Western music and musical education into all regions of its broad empire and sees to their adoption by means of political propaganda. Thus we find the Communist author Grigori Schneerson stating that "The ancient Chinese art of opera, closely linked with the ideology of Confucianism and feudalism, had cut itself off from life. It stood guard over the interests of the ruling classes . . . The great achievements and traditions of classical European culture helped the progressive musicians of China in their struggle against reactionary musical routiniers who were striving to isolate Chinese music from world culture and to press it into the frame of the canonical art of Antiquity."

Through this expansion the native art of primitive and oriental peoples is being driven back; by now it has largely died out or disappeared from the center of musical life. It has been or is being suppressed as an element in religious rites and feudal traditions and much of it is being pushed aside through the "war against illiteracy" and universal compulsory schooling; smothered, too, by Western folk and popular music and flooded out by the sound of the radio. Progressive industrialization of all parts of the earth will continue this process. Centuries ago the music of ancient American high cultures had died out, save for some bits remaining in folk tradition or a few instruments in museums. Elsewhere, in remote regions, or through tolerance, old traditions have been preserved. Understanding of their value and the wish to preserve them have grown in recent times, but destructive factors have also increased. Among primitive peoples and in the lower strata of oriental society music was largely interwoven in the forms of life; with the decline of these it is losing its previous meaning and reason. In a time of transition African Negroes who work in a factory or mine are able to take part in familiar dance and music-making in their time off, as they do at home; but these customs are doomed insofar as they cannot be fitted into the Age of industry and the museum—that is, either they are granted existence in the deliberate cultivation of folklore, the tourist industry, etc., or they undergo more marked alterations than ever.

For many peoples this violent overturn means an abrupt leap from forms of living in the First Age to those of the Fourth. Their own heritage and their own ways are still not entirely discarded, but remain as elements in various intermixtures, if sometimes only as vocal color or a characteristic execution of rhythm in the rendering of melodies of Western cast.

Occidental music could easily be assimilated by primitive peoples and the lower classes in the Orient because its popular forms, perfectly clear and simple, were intelligible to all. One such form is the plain eight-measure phrase in major with a steady alternation of tonic and dominant; it everywhere encountered more or less related structures and readily made itself at home. The "second primitivity" of such rhythmically simple melodic types meets original primitivity halfway: the very simplicity of a march or a lively *Ländler*-like Alpine *Schnadahüpfl* makes them striking and successful.

Melodies of this sort with correspondingly simple accompaniments are to be found all over the globe today (see music ex. 43). One hears them on reliable ethnographic discs of American Indians, even those from distant regions of the Amazon country, among Creoles of Bahia, the natives of the South Seas, in China, Korea, Borneo, and so forth. From the recordings and the notation of the music it is often hardly possible to tell that these songs and instrumental pieces are not being performed by Europeans.

Songs of South American Negroes to the guitar are scarcely to be distinguished from the run of recent Spanish pieces.

More frequently, however, the indigenous character comes through, with alterations. Research into the changes wrought in the singing offers a wide field of study that should cover not only certain songs but typical melodic configurations as well. On one recording, for example, Mexican Indians play music European in style, but in the drum rhythms something special shines through. One piece sounds like a classical Viennese cadenza formula, but in local usage it is repeated over and over like a line in a primitive song. Another disc gives the singing of a village community in Borneo on a festival night; it is in major with parallel thirds and sixths, but pentatonic underpinnings have remained.

In this process formular turns that seem stale to us may appear bright and fresh to those to whom they are new and represent the modern world. This holds true for march rhythms and choral pieces being spread by Sovietization. On records from Soviet republics, like Azerbaidzhan, Armenia, or Tadzhikistan, we hear choruses of robust political-march character, others with late Romantic chords and operatic effects, others again that alternate Russian and Arabic elements or mix original with a forced vitality.

Western music has everywhere entered into the high cultures of the Orient too, and concerts and radio broadcasting programs have been organized on the Western model. From Ankara to Tokyo, where a State Institute for the Study of European Music was founded in 1879, European music teachers are active and orchestras, choruses, soloists perform works of Mozart, Beethoven, Tchaikovsky. In Japan radio orchestras play Johann Strauss waltzes with sobbing sixths and pauses after upbeats, and a baritone gave Schubert's *Winterreise* on five consecutive evenings to a sold-out hall. In India the harmonium is widely used, and in Indonesia with the coming of the Portuguese in the 16th and 17th centuries indigenous traditions began to give way before light entertainment music "of superficial charm."

The folklorism, exoticism, and impressionism of Europe have prepared style mixtures that are now being carried further by oriental composers. From the Arab countries to the Far East native musicians are at work combining substance and color of their own with forms and ideas deriving from the West. Phonograph records show the most varied combinations: Israeli compositions with melodic material from the Yemen, Javanese gamelan orchestras tinted with Western harmony, Indian vina-playing with figures sometimes reminiscent of those characteristic of Bach's time, Chinese music with violins and bits of Western polyphony, a Japanese opera with European texture and timbres.

The meeting of Europe with Africa and with the American Negro at the beginning of the new Age has been rich in consequences: jazz, the Christian music of Africa, the Negro spiritual, South American dances are so far among the fruits of such interplay of influences. What fascinates us in the Negroes' way of singing and playing is not only their racial characteristics but also those archaic and universally human traits that take penetrating effect through their joy in playing and their power of expression. These traits come through, childlike and warmly vital, in the automatism of rhythmic movements, the intensity of the play of gesture. Pleasure in physical equilibrium, relief in sheer mechanical release, toying with the comic and the grotesque, as long ago in the use of masks—all these elements in man's essential nature are here thoroughly relished. Whoever seeks the mainsprings of music and dance will find them stronger here than in studiously cultivated folksong and artificial musical compositions.

New styles of Christian music have come out of the assimilation by these peoples, originally on religious grounds, of the Gospel; they differ in vitality from conventional church music, which uses local folklore but is largely composed on academic models and performed from score with a lifeless correctitude by Negro youngsters. Here and there, in elementary fashion bits of Gregorian melody mix with native ritual chant or, in the now famous American Negro spirituals, Negro tunes with Protestant chorale. This Christian Negro music was born under favorable stars. The Christian message has here, as a thousand years and more ago in Germanic and Slavic Europe, reached communities that have clung to religious values stemming from ancient and strong traditions, in contrast to those masses of mankind who have already lost these values through industrialization or Soviet-ization.

This interchange of influences has been looked into in writings about jazz, for example by Alfons M. Dauer. Jazz would prob-ably not have attained its world power if it had consisted only of a mixture of European harmony with Negro rhythms and manner of performance. Most important, indeed, is the way in which it combines elements of the First and Fourth Ages. Remodelling European structures into blues tonalities, hot intonation, swing rhythms, and using European instruments to quite different effect through a speaking, gesticulating, sometimes grotesque manner, it brought into play not only something specific to the Negro, but also something of a universal archaism. Primitive and refined at the same time, fusing the spirit of prehistoric man with that of today's civilization, jazz has spread irresistibly over the whole world. Everywhere there are groups active in the study of jazz (for example, dance get-togethers were announced "with jazz as a way to Heaven"). Courses in jazz are given in many music schools. In an article on "The Theology of Jazz," jazz is de-scribed as "a spiritual foundation" involving "the whole man, his whole emotional makeup," and by means of which rhythm is sanctified. In *Sovietskaya Kultura* it was recently argued that jazz was rooted in the folk art of the Negro and could be of good service in the education of the young.

The diffusion of jazz belongs among the counter-movements to the expansion of purely European music. In it one sees the changed situation at the beginning of the Fourth Age. What Europe has produced so far in our century in social dances is much too weak to fill the vacuum into which dance and music from across the Atlantic are streaming; European youth sings and dances whatever jazz, and the American popular-hit industry that exploits it, offers as a model. Other counter-movements against such European expansion are to be noted and expected: the setting up of further production centers outside Europe corresponding to the changing distribution of world power; com-petition to the point of superiority by non-Western musicians in the performance of Western music; the counter-influence on the

West of progressive Sovietization of musical life; national emancipation in Asia and Africa; criticism on the levelling and "monotonization" of the world. Yet through all these the fundamental character of this evolution seems only to be modified. The new Europe is despite everything much more alive than the prophets of doom have predicted, and the propagation of music chiefly from Western roots continues throughout the world. Its centers and its domains are growing in the whole of well-to-do society and, with increasing development aid, beyond such limits.

Progress in international circulation is broadening the range of musicians, who now travel by land, by sea, and by air, making possible a rapid succession of world music festivals, world congresses, world youth festivals, with participants from all parts of the globe. Tokyo is today nearer to Cologne than Prague was to Vienna in Mozart's time. And the radio "brings the world into your home," also for the inhabitants of thousands of scattered islands and far-lying countries.

In every branch of musical activity international associations have been formed, for music education, musicology, new music, folk music, and to link them all, the International Music Council. Through the organs of these groups and diverse other writings a world public is being built up. To it most of these publications are addressed and for it public activities in music are carried on.

Through the diffusion of compositions by means of printed music and recordings, in concerts and on the radio, a world literature of music has come into being that would have been impossible in Goethe's time, which saw the birth of world literature proper. Everywhere the same classical works form the basis of the repertory. In addition, present times favor world-wide uniformity in the most varied respects: the normalizing and standardizing of pitch, technique, terminology; the predominance of the same popular tunes and instruments in all parts of the world; and furthermore, everywhere unity of style in dodecaphonic and serial compositions that gives no clue to their country of origin. At the same time the new age favors mixtures and syncretisms: jazz in Arabic style for example, or French Catholic mysticism with Hindu ingredients. Efforts are also now being made to reflect the most varied cultural spheres side by side in a single work, much as Alessandro Poglietti did three hundred years ago when he combined in a set of variations "Bavarian shawms," "Hungarian fiddles," and other symbols of the countries making up the Austrian empire. Thus Dave Brubeck in his *Jazz Impressions of Eurasia* has worked style elements from England, Berlin, Poland, Turkey, India, and Pakistan into a suite (*Nomad, The Golden Horn, Calcutta Blues,* etc.), a work indicative of the global state of musical culture.

 3

POPULARIZATION AND DEPOPULARIZATION

Along with this global expansion there has come a second: the spread of music throughout all peoples, the democratization of musical life since the time of the French Revolution. As a result of this process, today far more than at any previous time popular entertainment music as well as works of musical art are offered to all classes of society by professional musicians. One aim for which philanthropists and friends of the people have striven seems to have been attained: the full range of music is now accessible to the entire population, everybody can hear, at least on the radio, practically anything he wishes to; the art is available to all.

The development of a "bourgeois" musical culture consisted not only in the replacement of one class of society by another but also in the change from a socially stratified to a common and democratic musical life. While music as an art had previously been largely limited, intended for closed circles in the ruling classes, it now became common property, public. For some time

indeed, the public concert was still tinged with bourgeois characteristics, but it addressed itself not only to a bourgeois audience
but to a public made up of members of different levels of society.
Whereas in earlier days musical compositions were performed,
when not in churches, for the most part in private—at court, in
aristocratic or patrician circles—they could now be heard by
anyone with the price of admission, and this, especially in the
more recent people's or youth concerts, was often small. This
process has gone further on the relatively classless—or middle-
class—level of today. The great majority of the population can
enjoy public performances of music as well as all the mass-
produced "post-bourgeois comforts of civilization," and because
of automation and the shortening of the workday is getting much
free time to spend in this way.

The diffusion of good music among the people and the initiation of the people into good music is furthermore being encouraged through social and national institutions. Humanistic ideas
such as Beethoven expressed in addressing his great works "to
Humanity" are here called to witness. The motives and organizations for mass musical education vary according to political attitudes, but this spreading of art among a nation's people is by no
means furthered only by socialist states; rather it is a general
trend of the times. In other countries too theaters, orchestras,
music schools are supported by state subsidy; the opera houses of
Germany, for example, which outnumber those of the rest of
the world put together. Names like "State Opera," "National
School of Music," have come to be taken for granted; so have
introductory courses in music appreciation for youngsters and
adults and so have requests for scholarships and grants for music
study. Yet this sort of thing is still comparatively new; it is one
of the particular traits that distinguish our time from all past
times.

Even more than through such social factors the general diffusion of music is being furthered through technological developments. Radio carries the greatest masterpieces "into every home";
music once limited to court circles, opera, orchestra, chamber
music are for the hearing of millions. The United Nations' annual

statistical report states that in 1959 the population of the world had risen to nearly 3 billion and of these 395 million were radio listeners. Add to this the phonograph record. In Germany every third household possesses a record player. In the United States $485,000,000 worth of long-playing records were sold in 1963; of which 13.8 per cent were classical music. The demand has increased not only for entertainment but also for education, culture, enjoyment of art. New categories of listeners and music-lovers have arisen: beside the masses who let themselves be constantly inundated, there are the anonymous lone listener to selective radio offerings and the passionate collector of good records.

The egalitarian trend that compulsory military service, compulsory schooling, and similar innovations in the life of the body politic were already maturing in the 19th-century prelude to the new Age, brought about categories of a new sort in popular music:

1) New types of popular song have appeared that are unlike the old-style folksong, and everybody sings or is obliged to sing them. National anthems and other songs that symbolize a whole nation or its dominant political party, have indeed lost, in the West, much of the importance attaching to them when first they flourished, but among organized masses, particularly those of the Soviet block, they are being systematically used. The "hit" song of unorganized masses, which had once flourished in late Antiquity, took on new life and new features through diffusion at first in cheaply printed editions and later by radio, cinema, juke-box. Preceded by the new kinds of song sung by professional folk singers in 16th-century towns and printed on cheap loose sheets, the modern popular song has evolved via carnival and operetta tunes to the present-day hit piece, which only became possible under the mass production methods of an industrialized society.

2) New on the horizon of universal history too and belonging to the Fourth Age is the development of musical societies. They differ from earlier types both in quantity and in organization. More and more surprising in the day of football and television fans is the great number of active members of choral societies—

in Germany in 1961 some 1,090,000. Add to this many thousands of brass bands, mandolin orchestras, etc.—again to cite West Germany alone with a membership of some 360,000. Many of the instruments used in this popular music were only invented in our century or the preceding: the mouth harmonica in 1821, for example, the accordion in 1829. Cultivation of such music is particularly advanced in socialist states of East Europe, China, and so forth, with their special political interest in the subject. In these countries as well as in America and Western Europe there is a growing number of symphony orchestras consisting partly or entirely of amateur musicians, that rise above the average of such popular lay activity. One would get a false impression of the real musical life of the present if one failed to emphasize this development so characteristic of it and which, despite setbacks, is going ahead in consequence of the increase in leisure time.

3) The largest place in the new Age, however, is taken by music for mass listeners, music that rises or attempts to rise from the most banal sort of entertainment to higher levels of popular taste. In the course of this development what might be called a popular edition has come into being for every genre of music, every type of musical performance: popular concerts, popular theater, popular opera, operetta, popular oratorio, and so on. The film, radio, television (though not yet available everywhere) were predicated from the first upon appeal to a vast public. The star system also, popular opera in the style of Puccini, and other forms often judged by mistaken standards, are all to be understood as resulting from the social structure of modern times.

From this structure too spring the attempts to continue composing works that inhabit several levels at once, appealing to both lay public and connoisseurs. Richard Strauss succeeded quite spontaneously in this, notably in *Rosenkavalier,* and after him Ravel, Honegger, Britten, Copland, and others have undertaken it with more or less success. For composers in the socialist states strict popularity has become a political norm; by its means they are to represent social progress, as in the West the avant-garde represents a purely artificial progress. "The new, young movement of progressive Chinese composers inflamed by the great ideas of Marxism-Leninism"—to quote Schneerson again—"is striving to serve the people, to speak in a language they understand and to train in them feelings of patriotism and national pride."

This whole process of popularization runs counter to the genuine folk traditions of the past. In the measure that today's popular music spreads those traditions fade, and vice versa. They have in fact not only been dying out since the industrial revolution, railroads, and radio, but began losing strength and variety several centuries earlier, as folksong melody levelled off into major tonalities, even rhythms, and regular verses, the spiritual folksong gave place in Protestant countries to congregational church singing, and the colorful multiplicity of customs allied to daily life and the round of the seasons became hollow and meaningless. This decline has been taking place, sooner or later and in varying tempo, in every country in the world.

Popularization plays a role, part positive, part negative, in the cultivation of folk music of the old sort, in the efforts being made to bring it back to a second life. It lies in the nature of the case that here different tendencies come to grips: some persons seek the widest diffusion of folksong and would wherever possible turn today's mass populations into a "singing people" again, and others strive to keep the genuine folksong pure, authentic, on a higher level, for limited though gradually widening circles, such as schools. The former type, insofar as they do not prefer to leave the radio on, sing *Silent Night, Holy Night,* the latter cultivate medieval Christmas carols. Even the countless composers who use folk tunes in large works attain only a limited popularity if the tunes are not really familiar to their listeners. It is something else again to offer the public peasant songs from remote countries re-written as properly composed pieces, as Bartók did, or old tunes from songbooks, as Hindemith did, or songs widely familiar to one's contemporaries, as Ludwig Senfl did four hundred years ago.

Together with advancing popularization, finally, a movement radically opposed to it is going on that corresponds to something similar in other arts. Everywhere the development has divided into extreme forms of popularity on the one hand, of esotericism on the other. Avant-garde music, through its atonal, athematic, anhedonistic principles, has passed out of reach of the lay public, and not only of conservative laymen but even of most amateurs. Its foundations are radically different from those of any secular music in any culture since prehistoric times. It departs from all popular appeal through its increasing artificiality and in expressly opposing mass production, the worn stereotype, cheap stuff. Music for the great public, on the contrary, quite deserted by composers of bolder spirit, falls to the more conservative and commercial powers. The one process brings about the other, popularization and depopularization promote each other. And paradoxically enough, the latter is only possible with the financial support of the great public—in the United States indirectly through the tax exemptions granted foundations and universities that sponsor avant-garde music, in Europe somewhat more directly in various ways, including government subvention of the radio.

In all its elements and all its forms new music has withdrawn always further from the approval of the many, in a direction quite contrary to that popularization which brought all types of composition within everybody's reach. In tonality, rhythm, form, content the more radical vanguard has become more and more artificial, appealing less and less to the understanding of a broader audience. The way in which those elements that please a large public disappear from a personal style, is shown, for example, by comparison of an early and a late work of Stravinsky, *Firebird* and *Agon*. Indicative of such depopularization are, beside most modern operas, the pieces Schoenberg entitles "Waltz" or "March," or Anton Webern's setting of ingenuous folksong texts like "Liebste Jungfrau" and "Schatzerl klein" (Opus 17 and 18). In his essay *Folkloristic Symphonies* Schoenberg disputed (both for the past and in principle) possibilities that have been realized from Haydn to Mahler. Adorno means something similar when he expresses not a historical judgment but a specific artistic intention: "After the *Magic Flute* serious music and light music have refused to be forced together . . . All 'light' and agreeable art has become illusory and mendacious." Hans Heinz

Stuckenschmidt has pointed out with special acumen this renunciation of popularity and democracy in composition: "We must build ivory towers. We must once more form small groups of the initiate who thrive on over-refined intellectual problems . . . I see among European youth a few creative musicians who have recognized that a highly exclusive experience of music is indispensable to the evolution of a culture. They attach themselves to the extreme forms of avant-gardist musical heritage. Their model is the highly introvert art . . . of Webern."

To see in this standpoint merely an arrogant contempt for the crowd—an *odi profanum vulgus*—and to think that only a better will is needed to reconcile audience and art, is to misconstrue it altogether. Arthur Honegger and other composers have indeed made an effort "to write music that should be comprehensible to the multitude and yet be so far free of the banal that it could captivate the real connoisseur as well," and in Soviet countries composers are constantly being reminded "to write music that combines the best craftsmanship and original and elevated quality with genuine appeal to the masses." But it is difficult, if not impossible, organically to unite really new styles of composition with folk tunes and other popular elements in so spontaneous a manner as Haydn and Mozart did. Attempts to mix twelve-tone technique with jazz elements, serial composition with touches that remind one of Puccini, merely combine what is incompatible.

RESUMPTION OF ALL PREVIOUS MUSIC
WHILE COMPOSITION EXCLUDES THE PAST

More than all earlier epochs ours is the age of old tunes that are dying out. But their dissolution has been preparing, they are not dying in the full vigor of life. In the words of the poet Georg Trakl, "At evening a carillon sinks away that sounds no more."

Folksongs are dying out and with them folksong itself, traditions are withering and with them tradition itself. This is especially true, though not without reservations, of that oral tradition which had already been pushed aside in Western music, but which outside Europe first began to languish and run dry in the Age of industrial civilization. With the disappearance of oral tradition freely varied improvisation also disappears; we no longer remold elastic models as folk singers did their songs or Arabic musicians their maqams, but reproduce musical compositions that have been set down once and for all in score or on records.

In other fields, too, naive tradition is pining away, and yet at the same time a conscious turning towards the past is on the increase, the "historization of the past, which obviously we can retain only as an image, not as a piece of our own life," as Reinhard Wittram says. The old bridges are replaced by new. Doubt is cast upon the veracity of our traditions about Beethoven and Mozart; we find it better to inquire of historical research how classical works were performed in their day and what consequences we may deduce therefrom.

With the exception of liturgical chant, music was made a subject of conscious preservation and history later than literature and the pictorial and plastic arts. During the 19th century the abundantly creative activity of Classic and Romantic masters filled the present, and performance of old music was markedly cultivated only in the church. Since the beginning of our century, however—after Arnold Dolmetsch had somewhat earlier revived the playing and making of old instruments, when Wanda Landowska brought the harpsichord to wider concert audiences—musical life has been filled as never at any previous time with works, forms, instruments of every period while the share of new compositions in the whole sum of performances has never been so small.

Musicology is casting its searchlights in every direction; manuscripts from all centuries are being collected, edited, published, folksongs are being gathered from everywhere, instruments from the world over—in brief, we are witnessing the revival of the musical heritage of all mankind. It is taken for granted that every possible discovery will be published, that even private letters and information on intimate details will be made accessible to the world at large. Formerly but little was known about the past and what was private remained private; but along the widening front of research, especially in biographical literature both within and without the domain of science, the veils are being lifted and every detail of our heritage is laid before the eyes of the world. In the time of Josquin, even of Bach, knowledge of the history of music was tiny as a molehill in comparison to the huge mounds of information contained today in a single encyclopedia of music in the past and present, like the great German *Die Musik in Geschichte und Gegenwart.*

Not only through the vicissitudes of changing preferences, but also in the sheer process of scouring all fields for material to collect have old masters like Lechner, Guillaume de Machaut, Perotin been revived. As for later masters, special branches of musicological research (Bach research, Mozart research, etc.) concentrate on establishing the original text, the correct style, the true aspect. Innumerable specialists find their life work in the study and performance of old music; indeed, most of the material gathered by ethnologists and folklorists is "old music." Composers like Bartók and Janáček are at the same time explorers in the service of historical knowledge.

Concerning the progressive diffusion of old music over the world Adalbert Kutz declared twenty years ago: "The great masters are known wherever technical civilization has taken hold in a metropolitan nexus. Negro boys in South African schools sing old English madrigals. The harpsichord renaissance, not yet thirty years old, is reaching out towards Cairo, Batavia, Singapore, Shanghai, or Tokyo." It is still difficult to extend the repertory in church, opera house, and concert hall, but radio and records offer almost unlimited possibilities of listening to music of all earlier periods, thus bringing it to life for a second time. A new section of that "world museum" which consists of the thousands of public museums and archives, libraries and record libraries of all countries, is being built out of a growing store of recordings: mankind's musical heritage in reproduction that is authentic or as nearly so as possible. That all recordings of serious music should be deposited in a central library of recordings is taken for granted; there is in fact some argument over whether it should not include all light and popular music as well.

Parallel to this extension over the world of the historic past goes progress in conscientious reproduction, and this is served by study of the history of performance as well as by the copying of old instruments. In movements like the renaissance of the organ other ideas and motives participate, indeed, but the basic purpose is to awaken all previous music to new forms of existence, forms that reach from a life on paper in a library or in the shadowy lodging of a museum showcase to high levels of revived understanding and performance.

Composers also, working in association with musicologists and performing artists, are taking possession of this historical heritage. Much as their tendencies, neo-classic or archaic, deviate from each other, they still have much in common that distinguishes their attitude towards history from that of earlier composers. Compare Stravinsky, Hindemith, Bartók with Bach, Mozart, Ockeghem in their relation to the music they inherited. How many more works of times both recent and long past today's composer knows in score and from performances, and how much his historical awareness has developed through contemplation of the distinctions between these periods!

Furthermore, in linking themselves to various historical moments and styles composers complement each other, much as specialists take on different aspects of a common problem and thus cooperate in some comprehensive historical task. For if one glances at the past styles they have heretofore followed, it becomes apparent that what they are utilizing and revivifying in their own compositions is the sum total of our musical heritage.

This includes in the first place, practically all styles of Western music in all periods, from the Classicism of the late 18th century, back through the phases of Baroque and Renaissance, to the Middle Ages: as witness Prokofiev's *Classical Symphony*, for example, Stravinsky's *Pulcinella* and *Apollon Musagète*, and his contributions to church music; also works of Malipiero, Pizzetti, Hindemith, Distler, Kaminski, Pepping, Orff, and others.

Secondly, there are the national styles, of the composer's own country and of other countries, the Western European and those whose traditions are still principally oral. "Only in our folk music," says Kodály about Hungary, do we possess "the organic continuity of our national heritage." And the same is true for folk music's part in national heritages in popular, artistic, and cultic music outside of Europe.

Thirdly, there is the deliberate cultivation of the archaic. Through the lack of written tradition from Antiquity, it is true, music finds itself in a position different from that of poetry or the plastic arts. At one time, as with exoticism, realistic models were replaced by imaginary conceptions when subjects from Antiquity—like Oedipus or Salome—were evoked in music: superhuman rigidity in declamation and rhythm was rather an imagined archaism than the archaic style itself. Again, archaic formulas and elements familiar from Christian cult music, are used to represent Antiquity; for example, recitative formulas against a background of primitive, not yet properly musical sounds in Orff's *Antigone*. Furthermore, elements borrowed from oriental and primitive peoples have for the most part archaic characteristics. Thus the asymmetrical "Bulgarian" rhythms of Bartók indicate, over and above the drawing from peasant music, the revival of rhythmic types evolved in the Second Age. Debussy and others were similarly reaching back to Antiquity and prehistoric times when they re-animated elementary forms of polyphony, of pentatonicism and tetratonicism. Through clothing such archaisms in new creative forms and combining them with imaginary versions of "chthonic and orgiastic," "magical and barbaric" music, prehistoric materials have been represented—for example, by Stravinsky in his *Sacre du printemps* or Prokofiev in his *Scythian Suite*.

It was the purpose of the self-confident adherents of such revivals to fill some particular old style with new life and carry it forward in a creative manner. But the accumulation of resuscitated styles verges on syncretism and eclecticism. The trends in question are no passing specialty of a few leaders choosing to borrow from the past but belong to the durable types of the new Age. Mersmann points out the "eclectic incorporation of the entire range of history including the 19th century" by the later Stravinsky and by Hindemith. Various works of Messiaen, in whose synthesizing of music of many times and peoples the idea of catholicity may well play a role, are most comprehensive in this respect. America and Russia have produced eclectic music of the most varied sorts.

Opera is particularly suited to exploitation of a multiplicity of styles, much as Thomas Mann in the novel or Bert Brecht in the drama juxtapose various linguistic styles from the Bible to the present day. This sort of combination belongs, like parody and travesty, among the more productive ways of handling historic styles. In the retention or remodeling of older forms, too, like rondo, ostinato, canon, the relatively fruitful transformations and altered meanings are to be distinguished from epigonous imitation. Stravinsky's sovereign and many-sided manner of manipulating all sorts of music is particularly comparable to the use of parody by Thomas Mann, who was with some exaggeration said to have no personal style of his own but simply a sublime way of handling the speech mannerisms of other persons and periods. Not only is what Thomas Mann himself called the "roguish parody" remarkable, but also that secondary productivity, as one might say, which takes as its base an aggregation of historical styles much as cantus-firmus settings once took the whole corpus of Gregorian melody. Even if in other shapes and other significances, the *cantus* or *stilus prius factus* has won new importance in the new Age.

Even though the possibility remains of once again bringing to life this or that music of the past, the series of first revivals in the manner of the Palestrina and Schütz renaissances may be essentially finished. The time of great discoveries of heretofore unknown types of music is also drawing to a close, just as the period of geographical discovery of new land is over; there are not many blank spots left on the map today.

In this changed situation the possibility appears of embracing the past as a whole. If not individually then collectively, historians, interpreters, and record manufacturers as well as composers are nearing the goal of a historical universality, so far as this is humanly possible. At the same instant this possibility has opened up for the first time in world history, however, there has arisen, and more urgently than ever before, the totally opposite challenge of completely breaking with the past.

Anti-conservatives today declare everything old to be obsolete, at least to the extent that it might become an ingredient of new creation. Going way beyond criticism of "historical fidelity" as a norm and the contempt of narrow-minded musicians for the music-historian's activity, they proscribe all clinging to the past as desertion of the avant-gardist cause. Whereas in every earlier master—a Josquin, a Bach, a Beethoven—conservative features were interwoven with progressive and with timeless or transhistorical elements, today the progressive element is picked out and elevated to sole importance in the whole and composition is supposed to exclude the past. The slogans and model ideas of progressive parties since the "Junges Deutschland," the "Young Germany" movement of around 1830, are carried further and, as in futurism, radicalized. History is a series of revolutions, ever new "conquests of the heretofore," "breaking of forms." The "canon of what is forbidden," according to Adorno, "today already excludes the resources of tonality, that is, those of all traditional music. Not merely that such sounds would be old-fashioned and untimely. They are false . . . The most advanced stage at which technical procedures have arrived sets problems over against which traditional harmonies show up as impotent clichés." This heritage itself demands that we do not resurrect it. According to Stuckenschmidt, the new situation places the artist "with no possibility of escape before the obligation to say what has never been said. It is his curse and his greatest blessing that he finds no more myths to hand. Only his own imagination can bring to birth works that, in Heisenberg's sense, confront man with himself. Today this is the profound meaning of the old theological concept of creation out of the void, *creatio ex nihil*." [1]

As has always been the case with earlier progressive parties, that of today is also calling forth reactions. Fearing obvious dangers rather than believing in ideological promises, many musicians plunge deep into the Western heritage. Toscanini, Furt-wängler, Hindemith became more conservative with age and turned back to the great masters and to what seemed to them eternal in music. Communism too, on the other hand, whether because or in spite of its progressive political intent, has turned away from artistic progress in the Western sense. Yet such reactions and regressions in their turn repulse those opposite progressive efforts and are the very thing actually provoking them into becoming avant-garde. "The more inevitably the fate of the epigone threatens," says Walter Jens, "the louder sounds the call to otherness. When all styles have been played out, the latecomer craves absurdities."

CONQUEST OF NEW TERRITORY; EXPANSION AND CONTRACTION TOWARD THE LIMITS OF MUSIC

To Paul Hindemith it once seemed "as though the sun had risen over a strange, shimmering, and radiant new land, into which musicians flung themselves like discoverers." This would be to compare the realm of music to a country of which composers were more and more taking possession, as the Europeans after Columbus occupied both Americas. Whether one assesses the

[1] "Eine neue Kulturepoche," *Melos*, 1959.

"thrusts into new country," the "expansion of the means of expression," the "conquest of the realm of tone," as a progress to something ever better, or otherwise, the reality of the process is not to be doubted. And together with the diffusion of music in all dimensions—geographical, sociological, and historical—this process is going on, one of the powerful expansions ushering in the Fourth Age.

Developments in Western music had in some respects reached their limits—for example, as in modulation from one tonality to another. Beyond the stage achieved by Richard Strauss, Mahler, Max Reger, new music had opened up new territory in rapid advances. Roused by the study of extra-European music and archaic folk music, it freed itself from the supreme control of major and minor, mastered the most various pentatonic and heptatonic modes and went on to reveal "anonymous tonalities," the whole-tone scale, chromatic scales, atonal and dodecaphonic structures. Similarly it passed beyond all traditional rhythms, mastering the most various possibilities of rhythmic asymmetry, labile diversification, forced motorization, syncopation, jerks and shocks. Since Debussy the logic of the harmonic cadence has been given up, the independence of stationary or fluctuating harmonies established, seventh and ninth chords freely moved throughout scale and chord passages, dissonances handled as values in themselves requiring no resolution. Every conceivable chordal combination was sought out and relished as an effect on its own account. Expressionism became absorbed in remote regions of the soul and of expression; like depth psychology, it explored uncanny borderlands of morbidity that had hitherto been avoided. Even in Scriabin this exploratory Expressionism was bound up with theosophical meditations, and on Schoenberg, Hauer, Webern esoteric speculations also had their influence. In early works, like opus 5 and 6, Webern was already realizing borderline values of subtlety and nuance in his articulation and instrumentation, his shredding of the fabric, his shifting interchange in dynamic and agogic degrees.

This rapid succession of innovations was based mainly on the intensive effort to create "the new," and a heretofore unheard-of persistence in pursuing the chosen aim as a chief duty and a chief standard of values. Like scientific and technical investigators, composers now practically set up a cooperative undertaking, as it were, for discovering and generating as quickly as possible ever new structures and sensations. Progress was unleashed; distrust of revolutionaries who could threaten a canonized cult or the poise of a culture, now became a mere sign of reaction, ideas involving "the quality of the familiar" were considered epigonous. Permanent revolution was taken for granted. Futurism made an ism of the future tense.

Busoni promulgated programmatic ideas preparing today's development, into which the new technical means are being incorporated in order to stimulate progress. "Exhaustion surely waits at the end of a course the longest lap of which has already been covered. Whither then shall we turn our eyes, in what direction does the next step lead? To abstract sound, to unhampered technique, to unlimited tonal material, I believe all efforts must be directed towards the virgin birth of a new beginning . . . Suddenly, one day, it seemed clear to me that the full flowering of music is frustrated by our instruments . . . In their range, their tone, what they can render, our instruments are chained fast, and their hundred chains must also bind the creative composer."

The advance of the virtuoso's technique to the point of perfection has indeed made possible much that seemed incredible before. What violinists or pianists, what choruses or orchestras would have been able fifty or a hundred years ago to master the difficulties today's composers expect them to master? But the new electronic means surpass the performing instrumentalist as motors surpass natural horsepower. Nowadays it is possible to execute everything imaginable in the way of intervals and distances, low and high registers, speed and intensity, color and dynamics. It will naturally take a little while before an electronic score is perfected, but from now on everything is possible in principle; the composer of today, like the astronaut and other technicians, is fulfilling the promise in the Garden of Eden: "Ye shall be like God," or of Nietzsche's Zarathustra: "I teach you Superman. Man is something that must be overcome." The limits set for the human voice and the executant hand are no limits for modern technique and composition.

Hence it might seem that in music too "the free use of the whole arsenal of technical means has," as Freyer suggests, "become an end in itself"; and that "our present culture," as Spranger puts it, "is the system of unlimited control over unlimited means." One might think our time the paradisaic hour for universal spirits who, being in full possession of all means, would now put to use the whole range of manifold possibilities they offer, as Wagner and Richard Strauss did in their day. But since Béla Bartók, the universal, who created a pedagogical *Summa musicae* in his *Mikrokosmos*, and Igor Stravinsky, the versatile, few composers have shown the will and the strength to achieve a synthesis. Among the leaders in serial and electronic music the drive to expansion in new territory is united with an equally strong impetus towards exclusion of all the accumulated wealth of the past, towards reducing music to composition that rests on the stilt-like scaffolding of an artificial world apart.

Thus progress becomes a departure. One does not win more land to add to what one has, but gives up the past in order to take possession of the new. "Consequences," says Schoenberg, "were drawn from an innovation that, like all innovations, destroys while it brings forth. We were presented with a new colorful harmony; but in the process much was lost." To say that every innovation destroys goes too far; in technology, in science, in art most innovations have only modified their heritage, not dismissed it. But the nature of some revolutionary systems is in fact exclusive. Whoever follows the rules of dodecaphony does not have the abundant possibilities before him that Bach or Wagner had with their chromaticism, but is surrounded by no-trespassing signs: no triads, no repetition, nothing that might bring into play tonality, which must be brusquely ousted. "Even a faint echo of the former tonal harmony would be confusing," says Schoenberg, "because it would call forth false expectations of implied consequences and continuity. The use of a tonic that does not depend on all the relationships of a tonality is fallacious." Serial and electronic composition too avoid the potential wealth of music that Mozart or Richard Strauss could so superbly utilize.

The new music adds, but it also omits. Never have the privative prefixes been so often applied. The supreme command, says Walter Jens, is everywhere reduction, not expansion. The reaction to cheaply luxuriant cultural activity is cultural asceticism.

The ideological justification of abstraction has produced many proscriptive formulas: something is "culinary," "warmly animal," "emotional stuffing," "narcissism," "bourgeois pathos." Stravinsky inveighed against the "nouveau-riche pomposity" of Wagner's *Gesamtkunstwerk* and its lush instrumentation. "The orchestra has become a source of delight quite independent of the music. We have had enough of this wallowing in thick sounds, one is tired of being satiated with tone-colors and no longer wants this overfeeding that distorts the whole musical element because it is blown up out of all proportion and given a life of its own." Such derogatory expressions belong to the style as the program belongs to program music. One misunderstands this abstinence if one does not remember the sidelong glance reflecting self-gratification that goes with it: We are not poor by necessity but of our own volition, we don't want profusion and bombast and façades, we want crystal clarity and unsentimental objectivity.

Music flayed, "l'art dépouillé," as Eric Satie said, can have its charm if only a few layers are peeled off; if nothing is left, the flaying is fatal. Actually, of the layers that constitute a fully musical work of art, one layer or another has been stripped away by different trends and in extreme trends almost all. The more music lost of its share in general connections like religion, home, style of living, the more of its corresponding properties vanished: aura, ethos, perspective, and so forth. Many immanent as well as transmusical values have succumbed. Esthetic isms have disavowed these values into the bargain, falsely invoking the example of the Middle Ages. Of a setting of the Credo, the confession of faith, a music critic, a believer, even says approvingly that "Stravinsky handles the text as phonetic material." Stravinsky himself has declared: "My view is that by its very nature music is incapable of expressing anything at all, whatever it may be, an emotion, an attitude, a psychological state, a natural phenomenon, or what you will." Yet as background and content of the musical work of art have been weakened or eliminated, so also have the strands of its fabric: the theme negated, harmonic logic, modulation, architectonics renounced. Now the tonal foregrounds or outer layers of the music were indeed peeled off.

In the process of reducing its supposed shackles, music was moving towards boundaries beyond which it is no longer music in the full sense of the word. But its expansion too came up against such boundaries. Conquest of new territory assumes that this territory already exists, as America existed before Columbus discovered it. Music is not a purely imaginary region that genius produces out of nothing, but by and large a realm of actual potentialities that are discovered and realized. When Boris Blacher writes variable meters—for example $\frac{12}{8}$-, $\frac{8}{8}$-, $\frac{7}{8}$-,$\frac{6}{8}$-, etc.—he has not invented these figures, their relationships and groupings, but has realized already existing possibilities. The realm of numbers is a sphere of objective possibilities given *a priori* which man exploits in music as in mathematics. The step from seventh to ninth chords was not created out of the void; it was a potential laid down in the system of possible chords. The more complex numerical relations are no less *a priori* than the simple; the relation $1 : 3 : 5 : 7 : 9$ was discovered, not invented.

But in so far as music is founded in a realm of preexistent possibilities that are realized little by little, the fact is to be reckoned with that the processes of realization do not go on ad infinitum, but come up against given limits, determined in the nature of things, in the same way as does expansion over the earth, over the strata of the population, over the historical world. The concept of "new territory" brings with it the problem of how far the new territory extends. This is not to say that the end of all composing is imminent, but that various processes that were part of the original realization of given elements and types of music are arriving at limits, just as the evolution of modulation within the major-minor system has reached limits, or as, while repeated revivals of old music may still take place, the series of original revivals of old styles is from now on entirely, or almost entirely, closed.

It is in fact characteristic of our time, of our phase of the Fourth Age in its beginnings, that most avant-garde styles should be moving towards border zones of music or passing over into the neighboring domains of language and noise. Musicology must investigate this exciting process objectively, without considering it treason if composers leave the realm of *ars musica* and settle in neighboring lands. In this investigation it will not accept any prohibition of independent thinking, but, wherever it exists as a free science, will recognize that to think independently is indeed its chief concern.

To prevent generalizing from the limits of some particular time-bound European style as though they were the limits set for all music, a prerequisite is to survey the subject from the point of view of universal history. We may leave aside the question of in how far the Greek conception of "muse" and "music" is binding in the matter of limits. It will be simpler to start from the definition of music as "the art of tones." This concept tells us, first that music is an art, and secondly that it is an art made out of tones.

1) As an art, by its very nature it brings intrinsic musical or transmusical content to a sensitive ear so that we feel it, understand it; when desensualized to a high degree it loses this character. The polyphonic structure in a good fugue, the thematic work in a good sonata, are audible to a suitable public or at least to connoisseurs of good will. But we approach one limit of the art if even such connoisseurs are unable to perceive a "row" and its transformations sufficiently well by listening and must resort to analysis of the score to establish it. Today, it is true, many achievements of some sciences—theoretical physics for example— have lost all relation to our senses, but such abstraction does not contradict the nature of these sciences; whereas in other disciplines—the writing of history, for example—a higher degree of descriptive clarity is essential, while art loses its character entirely if it ceases to appeal to the ear or the eye. Abstraction in music can bring with it values of its own and the result should not be dismissed as "paper music"; yet it does signify an approach to

the limits of music or a crossing of those limits.[1]

Music as an art, in the highest sense of the term, calls for an adequate standard of form. A musical work of art, for example a symphony, is more artistically constructed than other pieces, like potpourris. Various tendencies move away from this essential characteristic of artistic music: the primitivisms; music of severely pointillistic texture; extreme aphoristic music, which renounces the architectonic; the revulsion from constructivism to haphazard forms. Characteristic of the approach to this limit or the crossing of it is the following general injunction in a piano piece by Karlheinz Stockhausen: "The player looks casually at the sheet of music and begins with any group of notes his eye first falls upon; this he plays at whatever speed he prefers."

2) Music is the play of tones, that is, of fixed, clearly defined quantities. Other sounds, like glissandos, cries, noises, may occur as inserts; if they are numerous the result is partly musical; if they predominate, it is no longer music in the proper sense of the word.

A considerable number of modern works lie somewhere between song and speech. First came Schoenberg's *Pierrot lunaire;* other works followed, consisting partly of speech-song, whispers, cries, and even tongue-clicking. Rhythmic speech over a percussion ground provides the very impressive witches' scene in Carl Orff's *Bernauerin.* Elsewhere too, Orff in particular moves

---

[1] The deliberate ascetism of Schoenberg and composers who came after him has been characterized by Adorno: "Emancipated music casts suspicion upon all real sounds. Similarly, with the realization of the subsurface, the end of musical interpretation is in sight. Mute reading of music in our imagination could make playing aloud as superfluous as the reading of something written makes speaking it superfluous, and such practice could at the same time save music from the wrong that is done to it and its composer by almost every performance today. The tendency to mutescence, in the way it creates the aura around every tone in Webern's lyricism, is akin to this trend that began with Schoenberg. But this comes to nothing less than the result that emancipation and intellectualization in art, together with its material semblance, virtually wipe out the art itself. Emphatically the intellectualization of the art in Schoenberg's late compositions works at the dissolution of music itself and thus joins, in an abysmal coincidence, the barbaric element inimical to art." (*Prismen,* 1955, p. 210 ff.).

towards border zones between music and speech. As a way out of pure music, melodrama has taken on new significance.

A broader current leads from music to a sort of part-musical and also to a totally tone-free art of sounds. Already in the *Sturm-und-Drang* period of new music this current announced itself through the increase in percussion batteries and handling of the piano as a percussion instrument, and even then some composers were on their way to "noisism" (*bruitisme*). Diverse trends are carrying this current along: works for percussion alone or as accompaniment, use of pianos and other musical instruments "prepared" to give forth noises, "musique concrète," and above all the electronic generation of "artistic" noises (which indeed often remind one of natural noises and their sources). The various possibilities are also combined: thus in his *Kontakte* (1960) Stockhausen intends to give traditional timbres new qualities through association with electronic sounds.

Discussion about the nature of the new art of sounds, those part-musical and those totally untonal, is beclouded by the fact that it is called concrete or electronic "music." Three problem areas, often confused, must be distinguished: firstly, defining and differentiating between the art of tones and the art of sounds; secondly, determining the value and the developmental possibilities of the new art of sounds, especially whether, like the game with tones and their logical combinations, it can be made into an independent art; and thirdly, specific inquiry into the relationships between tone and tone-free sound in the universal history of mankind. Some points of contact between the primitivism of prehistory and that of today are obvious. This exodus from the realm of music corresponds in reverse direction to the historic transition from pre-musical and part-musical forms into the realm of music. Yet it would be an exaggeration to see in these analogous movements the beginning and the end of music.

TECHNICIZATION AND ARTIFICIALIZATION

What is "technique" and "technical" in music? In Antiquity the general term for music as an art was "technē mousikē." Some musicologists call devices in medieval composition "techniques." In a more specific sense one speaks of "piano technique" for virtuoso facility upon that instrument, and correspondingly with other instruments. Around 1800 instrumental technique received a fresh impetus; a particular type of composition appeared, the "étude," and concertizing musicians began to work up their dexterity through forced practice until it became automatic to a high degree. In the sense that today is the age of technique, however, it is only a few decades ago that the art of music itself became technicized, and that in a double manner: first through application in the field of music of the technical spirit of engineering, and secondly, through electronic production and transmission of sounds—the disc, radio, electronic composition, and so forth.

1) How the new spirit of technicization, with the ideas and attitudes evolved from it, has spread over various fields, has been set forth by Hans Freyer, Arnold Gehlen, and other writers. This spirit has also affected a part of today's production and reproduction of music by traditional means. It is behind the perfectionism of soloists and orchestras, and many ways of performing music aim at an expressionless "objectivism," following directly the model of machinery set in motion and whizzing through its task, even though there is often a spiritual superstructure here that justifies the automatism.

Technical patterns and procedures, furthermore, permeated a

good deal of pre-electronic composition. "Play this piece very savagely, but always severely in rhythm, like a machine," says an instruction of the young Hindemith. He and other composers who were trying to transform models of Bach's time in the spirit of the technical age combined the motorization of rhythm with restless continuity into a new sort of *perpetuum mobile* in sound. Technomimicry in music could serve to represent railroad trains and other machines, or people would hear such content into the music.

In constructivism the new technical spirit worked together with increasing artificiality. The so-called tricks of old Netherlands origin, like horizontal and vertical inversion, were taken up again in a new polyphony, particularly in dodecaphony, and overdone. The serial movement carried this process into a structure consistent throughout, arranging in "rows" not only successions of tones but rhythm, dynamics, articulation, and other musical elements. Since here construction dominates as an end in itself, it does not matter if the listeners cannot perceive it or if they think so little of it that they would rather spend their time on other intellectual occupations. Like all tendencies of the present, this too was given an ideological superstructure. Thus Ernst Krenek asks: "Is composition then reduced to the filling out of a given, serially calculated scheme? Instead of seeking points of escape that might make the matter more toothsome to the taste of a tradition-conscious public it is fairer to answer the question with a simple 'Yes!'" Heinrich Strobel finds increased artificiality the very thing that determines the essence and the worth of all modern art. "Artificial is a consequence of *ars*, a not 'artificial' art is simply no art . . . Art, like everything intellectual, is sustained by the minority. The creative minority in our century has carried out a magnificent achievement: it has passed beyond the natural arts . . . In music this means turning away from the naturalistic principle of tonality, from rhythmic symmetry, from the thematic scheme. Thinking in terms of sonority has taken the place of tonal painting of pictures and states of soul."

2) A difference that runs deep between the Fourth Age and

all earlier epochs is due to its electro-acoustical discoveries. These discoveries tumble the old foundations and lay new ones: musical life has in large measure changed, former types of sound are reproduced in altered fashion, new artificial types are being created, and over and above this, music has taken on new forms of objectification. The evolution to records and other transmitters is no less great than the change that brought about the notation of music in score; and it is taking place much faster.

a) On records, magnetic tape, and film musical works are not—as in a score—set before us to sing or play, but are presented to us already fully sounding. Records of different performances of a symphony show the work under different aspects. The works themselves are much more easily accessible than heretofore and in greater number, and they are preserved "forever." A *phonothèque* is a cross between a library and a museum. It contains many copies in sound of a smaller or larger treasury of musical works, and the universal phonothèque towards which the development is heading could ideally embrace all surviving musical works from all times and peoples in authentic recordings or reproductions. In addition, thanks to these new bearers of tone, the performing musician has the chance that his own performance will live on in the world. Similarly, all oral traditions from all parts of the earth are in this way objectified in new forms of existence, whereby most of them skip the stage of written notation.

b) Radio and television wipe out space, and bring the greatest of masterworks into the smallest of huts. One lets oneself be inundated by plugged-in music and goes walking with one's transistor. A great many people in all parts of the earth have seen and heard a great many operas, but not a single one in a theater; they hear all the instruments through artificial transmission, but rarely any in their natural timbre.

c) New electronic instruments in part latch on to traditional instruments and attempt to reproduce their tone by more economical means, substituting electro-acoustic mechanisms for organic materials like soundboards, pipes (organ), tubes (wind instruments) and modifying the method of playing accordingly (electronic organs, claviolins, cembalets, etc.) or aiming at the production of new timbres (like the trautonium). In the imitations of genuine instruments not only does the resulting tone deviate more or less from the original, but above all the very act of making music is altered. The more important it is to consider not only the sounds produced but also the playing itself and its value in education, the more the imitation remains *Ersatz*.

d) Electronic apparatus for measuring and recording, reproducing and generating sounds is altering the task of theoretical and practical musicology. In a short time a whole series of special institutes for experimental study of new possibilities in understanding and practice has come into being—for example, Hermann Scherchen's Electro-Acoustic Experimental Studio in the Swiss village of Gravesano, near Lugano (1954). We may count on many more such institutions making systematic advances in the process of technicization.

e) It has become a hobby to alter, mix, or make sounds on a simple magnetic tape recorder. The playback makes it possible for a single individual to record a vocal trio by singing one part after the other on the same strip of tape; or, in the same manner, to play a piece for piano four-hands with his own two. These simple, domestic achievements are far outdone by the technical manipulations possible in a studio. Sounds are altered by leaving out now this, now that band of the tonal spectrum, by reducing and synchronizing, by modifying the echo and other spatial and auditory acoustic effects, splitting tones and generating them synthetically through various sinusoidal combinations. The new technique, says Freyer, "generates synthetically materials with desirable properties unknown to nature, artificially building large molecules. It thus increasingly frees itself from natural growth and accretion." As in general "the makeability of things is being carried to the point of molecular construction of materials, so too the elements of music are not being taken from nature but artificially produced." The realm of tone and clang becomes mere material, with which *homo faber* does as he pleases. Intrinsically, says Heinrich Strobel, "the material of sound has neither form nor character. Both are bestowed upon it by thinking man"—more exactly, the composer or the program annotator.

f) Of the attempts to create electronic musical compositions out of artifical tones and timbres some scarcely go beyond traditional sounds and content despite the new means, while the more radical seek the unprecedented even in such material. Stockhausen and others manipulate language as they do music, transposing a boy's voice, for example—as Stockhausen does in his *Gesang der Jünglinge (Song of the Youths in the Fiery Furnace)*—into various registers, deleting formatives, taking consonants apart and leaving only shreds of the wording so that it can be understood. A biblical text here becomes material for the generation of new sounds. In the corresponding ideology the genuineness of this process is set over against the surrogate character of reproduction on records and its progress beyond all earlier natural methods vaunted: "The first step to real musical control of nature," says Herbert Eimert, "has been taken by electronic music. Its dependence for reproduction on the loudspeaker—which moreover has brought about an as yet scarcely noticed subterranean revolution in hearing—at last permits risking the hypothesis that the symphony fixed on disk or tape may be the surrogate and electronic music the true music. Here, we may surmise, is the point at which the true order of music is revealed."

ORGANIZATION, INDUSTRIALIZATION, AND IDEOLOGIZATION OF MUSICAL LIFE

The technical forms and constructivist styles in music of the new Age are "secondary structures" that *homo faber* has erected over the former natural ways of making music. Other secondary structures have grown up alongside them that are also much more artificial than corresponding aspects of musical life heretofore. They form the modern lattice-work of apparatus, industries, officials, functionaries, ideologies, copyright arrangements, and so forth, which overlay the Muse's part in music and often suppress it, although they are particularly set up to take care of it.

As in all cultural areas, the new Age is distinguished from all earlier Ages in music too by the enormous number and importance of its organizations. Whatever is organic is in part encouraged by them, in part tolerated, in part organized away. The number of societies and institutions has multiplied and the number of activities, especially congresses and festivals, also. The title "music festival" is inherited from the 19th century; the sessions themselves have little festive character.

Where the totalitarian state and economic planning dominate, the pressure increases and the lattice-work is tightened through rules and regulations. Music is placed at the service of political schooling and propaganda. In other parts of the world cultural liberalism makes for a counterpoise, though here new types of organization make possible esoteric tendencies which in concert life, in a "free market" or other areas based on natural supply and demand are not viable. Since in some countries the key positions in mass organizations like radio, publishing houses, newspapers, and governing boards are to a large extent occupied by professionals who are leaders or fellow-travelers in esoteric movements, this music receives plentiful support and encouragement. The term "Macaenas" is scarcely applicable in this situation.

Further secondary structures have arisen in the modern music industry. As a consequence of new techniques, popularization of music, and lengthening of leisure time it belongs among the industries with the greatest financial turnover. This holds for the production and circulation of popular hits, records, popular instruments, phonographs, automatic players. Specifically industrial features appear not only in the type of manufacture and adaptation to the mass of paying customers, but particularly in the advertising with which hits are launched, demands covered or artificially worked up. Slogans promise "music to dance and dream to," "the world in your home," "with our superautomatic you are never lonely." Art music, church music too, are extolled by new methods if not often with new expressions: "Our Golden Record Album simply belongs in your cozy home. In the dusk of evening's approach, comfortably installed in your armchair or on the sofa, you will peacefully enjoy the immortal music of Mozart, Liszt, or Schubert. Light a candle whose quiet light will shed an aura of romance upon the festive hour. You've been wanting this for a long time!" "We consider it important to catch and cultivate the interest of our young people in the music of their time. The Negro spiritual is perfect for this. The present selection, designed for the schools, will also appeal to youth groups and choruses if they are open and ready . . . Let us give our youth spirituals. They want them, and they'll convince us too!"

Ideologies are not ideas, plain or abstract, but intellectual supports for secondary systems. They may include knowledge, but in the measure that new knowledge might be unfavorable to the trend or party to be advocated, they are inimical to the will to know. "In New Music circles also," says Adorno, "the enunciation of recognized truths is sabotaged, the implication being that they might benefit the opposition." In the new Age music is conditioned and accompanied as never before by ideological cogitations. Programmatic writings, reviews, criticisms, commentaries, and school courses are not extras one could do without; they are necessary to make possible the secondary system they sustain. They consist in large part of putting a few motifs and popular topics through their paces, such as: audiences are accustomed to comfortable enjoyment of traditional music and are too set and too lazy to understand anything new; the dissonances that scare the ordinary citizen are expressive of his own condition and only for this reason are intolerable to him; there are many tonal systems in the world that have nothing whatever to do with tonality; no composer of new-style music has ever put himself across until late; efforts on behalf of electronic music are the musical parallel to atomic research, in which the spirit of our time is concentrated. In this fashion various secondary structures—constructivism, organization, ideology—are bracketed fast together, for which reason they may remain viable for a long time.

BETWEEN DEHUMANIZATION
AND REGENERATION

To the extent that man is by nature *homo faber* and technical inventor, he is realizing himself in the age of technique more fully than heretofore. To the extent that progress and change are characteristic for him, the permanent revolution at the beginning of this Fourth Age might be regarded as an intensification of his nature; avant-garde composers, according to Hermann Scherchen, see it as their mission "consciously to develop man's organs in a new and finer way." Yet from another point of view the detaching of music from man is an unmistakable feature of the time. Many trends even prescribe and promote this separation. "Where para-artistic enterprises use humanity as a pretext for commerce in esthetic fields," says H. H. Stuckenschmidt, "it is better to take one's stand on the side of inhumanity. Since totalitarian dictatorships have discredited the concept of the human, one should at least keep it out of the domain of the arts."

How far dehumanization goes does not become clear until we glance at its different aspects. To begin with, there is replacement of the performer by apparatus. Singing and playing oneself, at home, has diminished; unlike the time around 1500 or 1800, today's avant-garde do not write for the lay music-lover; and besides their works are mostly too difficult for the amateur and do not attract him. Many of the new compositions ask too much of the professional musician whose function in them is only partial, not involving his whole personality; Stravinsky wanted him to be no more than the bell-ringer who sets the bell sounding. In electronic works he has no share whatever; technicized composition has no need of him.

Even the listener in this technical Age plays a far from fully human role. Much more than ever before the organized concert and opera public leaves to others the intitiative and preparation for what it is to hear. For the radio listener preparation is reduced to the turning on of his machine. It is made difficult for the public to develop its own taste and independent judgment, and public opinion is taken care of by professionals of the press. Music inundates the consumer masses and provides a surge of sound as background to reading the newspaper or doing homework. Carried to extremes, the radio needs no listener at all; the music is broadcast at the stated time, even if there is no one to take it in.

New compositions do without the human voice or handle it like an instrument or denature it through electronic manipulation: Stockhausen's *Gesang der Jünglinge* is a model of dehumanization. At the same time the "natural orders" and their play of harmonic equilibrium, on which the idea of *musica humana* rests, are eliminated, and particularly those musical structures that correspond directly to man's psycho-physical organism, like pulsating rhythm, plastic melodic forms, and the periodic alternation of systole and diastole.

Furthermore music is dehumanized by the suppression of the chief subject of most earlier music—man, a psycho-physical whole—the stunting of relations of fellowship and mutual exchange (between musician and audience because of technical intermediaries, between the composer and his world generally) as well as by the loss of all former sense of music as something possessed and inherited. Music is finding itself homeless; disseminated without hinderance, it now belongs only in secluded areas, like monasteries, or functioning, as at Christmas, at given times and places in an ordered life. Become jejune and dreary through technicization, most of its possibilities of taking part in life have vanished. Work songs cannot thrive in factories, nor any musical atmosphere form about an industrial metropolis, as it once could in Nuremberg or Venice. The church bell was a symbol of old cultures; a symbol of industrial culture is the factory siren.

There is in our new Age, however, continual criticism of "dehumanization with all the comforts" (as Freyer calls it) and threatened values are being newly appreciated; when everybody else is glued to the television, we find an oasis wherever amateurs make music themselves. People seek areas of compensation, musical sprees, improvised jazz, rock'n'roll—some spontaneous, some planned—in which they can be more humanly active, have their fling more freely than in the centralized zones of a mechanized and organized consumer society. Regenerative movements are under way, too, that link back to those of the *Sturm-und-Drang* period, to Romanticism and youth-movements. Distinct from such utopian efforts at romantic revival there are realistic endeavors going on, very similar to the movements in urban and landscape planning which, now that the period of industrial communities with their seas of houses is past, are introducing green areas into the cities and surrounding them with garden communities. Musical education and cultural policy are developing as a necessary counterbalance in the Age of dehumanizing technique. In addition there are fresh efforts to explore the uses of music in physio- and psychotherapy and in the corresponding medical education.

Apart from utopian attempts at reform, the advantages of making music for oneself are exploited under the slogan of "do it yourself." Countries particularly advanced in industrialization, like the United States, also develop particularly strong countermeasures. Thus different spontaneous trends are moving in the same direction—the awakening to musical experience and activity in kindergarten, a considerable part of jazz activity, the upsetting of constructivist principles in compositions that leave great freedom to the preference of the individual performer.

The insights of modern psychology and ethnology point to a restoration of the human; the unity of all music throughout the whole of humanity, preformation of the perceptible world, "natural orders" that underline all musics. The cognitions of psychology, Gestalt and Complex, for which Christian von Ehrenfels prepared the way using melody as a model and which Wolfgang Köhler, Max Wertheimer, Felix Krüger, E. M. von Hornbostel developed, have been carried further by the work of Wolfgang Metzger, Albert Wellek, and others. They contribute to a new foundation for music theory and education.

The forces of dehumanization and regeneration work concurrently, with and against each other. The neo-romantic movements have lost momentum and gained in realism. They have mingled with developmental traits against which they once took the field—"museumizing," for example; but in return their ideas have worked out to the benefit of school, church, organized musical activity. Radio music and home music are not opponents only, but partners as well, as, for example, when special radio programs effectively stimulate people to play themselves. Exhortations to return to the past are illusionary in face of the massive powers of the new Age. Really to overcome dehumanization or confine it, the more realistic forces seek to carry on the idea of renewal in such a way that it may become an effective counterpoint and counter-balance to the cantus firmus of technique.

PROGRESS OR END?

Through the 19th and 20th centuries ran trends aiming directly at progress. Different in content as the "futurism" of Busoni and our own "avant-gardism" may be from Wagner's "music of the future" and the "progressive party" of his day, still in their concept of historical becoming they are carrying on these earlier trends, forcing them forward. One utopia follows upon another. Thus Busoni proclaimed that "only a long and conscientious experimentation, a continuous educating of the ear, will make this unaccustomed material tractable to a growing generation and to art. What fine hopes and visionary perspectives are wakening for them!" Such utopian aims and the belief that one is of the vanguard are basic to the solidarity of parties conscious of their time. "The new!" becomes a slogan as "Kyrie eleison!" did once. A religiously irreligious passion drives creative composers and their adherents ahead into the future, as once it drove earlier spirits to absorb themselves in the Eternal.

Yet however much the will to progress grows and stiffens, a number of facts indicate that it no longer altogether corresponds to the present stage of evolution. It has become clear that in music there are no longer infinite stretches of new territory open to conquest, that its expansions have come up against boundaries or must pass over these boundaries into neighboring realms of noise. For the creating of ever new modes, rhythms, harmonies, polyphony, and so forth, the same thing holds as for the revivals of old music and for the spread of music over the globe and the masses of its population. The present successors to the avant-garde are actually so few that it is doubtful whether they could be called avant-garde in the proper sense of the term. The utilization of the border zones of music and the human soul leads to particularly severe attrition; what was once intended to frighten and to shock has become "cooled-off material." Moreover, up to now only a few new works have been incorporated into the permanent repertory of concert halls and opera houses. In consequence, the position of today's composers has deteriorated in comparison to that of performing musicians and conductors. It is by no means a matter of course that the composer should at all times be as much a leader in the shaping of musical life as he was from Josquin to Bartók.

Hence it is not surprising if Arthur Honegger, in his book *Je suis compositeur*, is convinced of the decline of the art of music. "Our art is leaving us and disappearing. I fear that music will be the first to leave us. The further I advance, the more I realize that it is releasing itself from its own destiny: from the charm, the wonder, the solemnity that should aureole artistic revelation." Thomas Mann, in *Doctor Faustus*, and other authors too, have expressed the doubt already suggested by Hegel and Beaudelaire about the future of art. To every side has spread a weariness of progress, a weariness of history.

Yet back of this alternative between avant-gardism and pessimism ideas are stirring that Ernst Jünger has formulated as "entry into the trans-historic world." Inadequate as such formulas are, they point to a change in the structure of historical becoming. Profound alterations have taken place in it before; the high cultures, late Antiquity, the Middle Ages, Modern Times—they differ not only in what happened, but in how it happened. Progressive conquest of new territory is a particularly important mode of historical becoming, but it is not the only one. This pattern of thought does not do justice to much of importance that has happened in the past and in the present. Thus Béla Bartók's late works represent not a going forward towards the future but a deepening in another direction. What was once called eternity is more than a plain illusion. Schoenberg's late works, like his Fourth String Quartet, or Alban Berg's Violin Concerto, are not to be understood as inspired primarily by the idea of continuation along a single-track line of progress, any more than are the particularities of an Orff or a Distler, or the efforts to deal with liturgical music and *Gebrauchsmusik* with the immediate situation in mind rather than with progressive intent. The history of composition may unfold in a steady line of progress, like the history of science, but it may also go from one high point to another, just as the history of philosophy moved on, indeed, from Plato to Kant and Nietzsche, but made no actual progress. It is not unreasonable to think that in future the history of musical composition may proceed in this second mode of historical becoming rather than in the first.

So far as any prognostication is possible, it presupposes diagnosis of the present and insight into the course of past history. Our survey of music history in its entirety has revealed evolutionary features that began partly in prehistoric, partly in later times, as for example the artificialization of instruments or the decline of oral tradition as it was pushed aside by script and later by techniques of recording. It is to be assumed that these lines of development will continue and we may picture the future to ourselves in so far as we imagine them extending on beyond the present. Yet some lines, as we have seen, come up against limits beyond which they cannot go. And we cannot foresee how far the counter-movements against them will carry—for example the tendency toward regeneration against the trend to dehumanization. Even if we think we know how the opposing forces are made up, we do not yet know what will be the results of the battle between them.

Another established point significant for a diagnosis of the present and for prognosticating further developments concerns the historical differences in all music heretofore. After a passing modern trend that took into account only divergences in styles, today's comparative musicology is finding alongside the differences a considerable number of common features in the substructures of all times and cultures, just as in present-day general anthropology the traits common to all mankind appear to be greater than many authors of Lévy-Brühl's day assumed. And herewith light falls upon the position in history of the radically new directions in composition today. In their style as in their attitude toward the contemporary public they appear to be exceptional, a unique phenomenon when compared with all other times and cultures. This helps to explain why they have heretofore persisted only in small circles of specialists, and it points to the likely limits of their future reception.

Yet a pessimistic prognosis would be just as little founded on fact as an optimistic one. As in the present, so too in the near future music will be living a life extraordinarily rich and multiform. Surely many compositions will be produced and among them important ones, but probably the view will again grow stronger that the substance of a culture is not exhausted in what it produces, that the culture itself consists of something more than the possession of works of the past and the begetting of works for posterity. In the last hundred years ideas came to take command that had not existed before or that in music had not fully developed: creating for posterity, serving a common progress, and the steadily continuing conquest of new territory. Will these ideas keep their force, or will perhaps other ideas, which during this time have been repressed, become effective in some new way: the culture of life itself, the fulfillment of the moment, and together with these a turning toward what is eternal in music?

APPENDIX

SOURCES OF THE MUSIC EXAMPLES

1. Taken down in 1907. Max Wertheimer, *Musik der Wedda*, in *Sammelbände der Internationalen Musikgesellschaft*, XI (1909), 302, No. 2.
2. Jaap Kunst, *De inheemsche Muziek en de Zending*, Amsterdam, 1947, p. 29.
3. *Notes sur la musique des Bochimans, comparée à celle des Pygmées Babinga* . . . , recording of the Peabody Museum and the Musée de l'Homme, with commentary by Y. Grimaud and G. Rouget, p. II.
4a. P. L. Kirby, *A Study of Bushman Music*, in *Bantu Studies*, X (1936), 205 ff., Ex. 11; M. Schneider, *Ethnologica, Neue Folge* 2 (1960), 433 ff.
4b. K. Tirén, *Die lappische Volksmusik*, Upsala, 1942, No. 19.
5a. Same source as Ex. 3, p. I.
5b. and c. Same source as Ex. 4b, Nos. 465 and 50.
6a. F. Densmore, *Menominee Music*, in *U. S. Bureau of American Ethnology Bulletin*, 102 (1932).
6b. Robert Lach, *Gesänge russischer Kriegsgefangener*, in *Sitzungsberichte Wien, Philosophisch-historische Klasse*, 204/V (1929), 45, No. 110.
6c. F. Liuzzi, *La Lauda e i primordi della melodia italiana*, 1934, I, 387.
7a. G. Rhaw, *Bicinia*, 1545, No. 84.
7b. Nils Andersson, *Svenska Låtar*, I, 1922, No. 384.
7c. M. Schneider, *Kaukas. Parallelen zur mittelalterlichen Mehrstimmigkeit*, in *Acta Musicologica*, XII (1940), 57, No. 3.
7d. Y. Matsudaira, *Seven Japanese Folk Songs from Nambu District* (Tokyo, 1937), in *New Oxford History of Music*, I, 146.
8a. *Chanson d'Audigier* from the *Jeu de Robin et Marion* of Adam de la Halle; see F. Gennrich, *Der musikalische Vortrag der altfranzösischen Chansons de geste*, 1923, p. 10 ff.
8b. A. D. Grigoriev, *Archangelskiya byliny*, I, 1904, p. 661, No. 10.
9a. A. Z. Idelsohn, *Gesänge der jemenitischen Juden*, 1940, p. 87.
9b. *Editio Vaticana*.
10a. A. Z. Idelsohn, *Gesänge der babylonischen Juden*, 1922, p. 89.
10b. *Editio Vaticana*.
11a. A. Bake, MGG, VI, article *Indische Musik*, col. 1157.
11b. Idelsohn, *Gesänge der jemenitischen Juden*, p. 54.
11c. P. Wagner, *Einführung in die gregorianischen Melodien*, III, 1921, 60.
12a. A. Bake, *loc. cit.*, col. 1160.
12b. Idelsohn, *Gesänge der babylonischen Juden*, p. 98.

12c. *Idem.*, p. 91.

13a. E. Felber, *Die indische Musik der vedischen und der klassischen Zeit*, in *Sitzungsberichte Wien, Philosophisch-historische Klasse*, 170/VII (1912), 101, No. 39.

13b. *Editio Vaticana.*

14a. A. Lavignac, *Encyclopédie de la musique*, I, 1922, 2819.

14b. H. Anglès, in *Archiv für Musikforschung*, III (1938), 360.

15a. V. Stoin, *Narodni pesni ot Timok do Vita* (*Chants populaires bulgares du Timok à la Vita*), 1928, No. 935.

15b. S. Trébucq, *La Chanson populaire et la vie rurale des Pyrénées à la Vendée*, 1912, II, 47.

15c. *Antiphonale*, 1935, p. 202; MGG, I, col. 341 ff.

16. After A. Tobler, *Kuhreihen, etc. in Appenzell*, 1890, p. 53.

17. Same source as Ex. 11b, p. 107.

18. Lavignac, *op. cit.*, p. 3082.

19. A. H. Fox Strangways, *The Music of Hindostan*, 1914, p. 299.

20a. E. M. von Hornbostel, in *Archiv für Musikwissenschaft*, I (1918–19), 484.

20b. *Le MS dit des Basses Danses . . .* , ed. E. Closson, 1912, No. 28.

21. Op. 117, No. 4, *Sämtliche Werke*, 24, p. 110.

22. Béla Bartók and A. B. Lord, *Serbo-Croatian Folk Songs*, New York, 1951, p. [104].

23a. After M. Schneider in *New Oxford History of Music*, I, 66, No. 46.

23b. M. Schneider in *Zeitschrift für Ethnologie*, 70 (1938), 304.

23c. Facsimile in C. Sachs, *The Rise of Music in the Ancient World*, 1943, facing p. 193.

24a. H. Weil and T. Reinach, *Bulletin de correspondance hellénique*, 17, 1893; *The History of Music in Sound* 8/15 and [32] f.

24b. W. P. Malm, *Japanese Music*, Vermont and Tokyo, 1959, p. 97.

24c. From the madrigal *Dulcissima mia vita*, Madrigal V. Barred as in the original printed score, 1613; see A. Schering, *Geschichte der Musik in Beispielen*, 1931, No. 167.

25. Universal Edition 12 398.

26a. Fox Strangways, *op. cit.*, No. 197.

26b. Lavignac, *op. cit.*, p. 2979.

27a. Stoin, *op. cit.*, No. 2593.

27b. *Musica Nova. Zeitgenossische deutsche Musik auf Schallplatten*, Serie 1956, score p. 63.

28a. From the Mass *Se la face ay pale, Opera omnia* III, 1951, p. 2.

28b. *Parsifal*, Introduction.

29a. From *Cardillac*, first version. Used as an example in Wörner, *Neue Musik in der Entscheidung*, 1954, p. 25.

29b. Bärenreiter Edition, No. 3330.

30a. Marius Schneider, *Contribución a la música indígena de Matto Grosso (Brazil)*, in *Anuario Musical*, VII (1952), Ex. 32.

30b. The same, Ex. 30.

31. Marius Schneider, *Geschichte der Mehrstimmigkeit*, I, Ex. 129.

32. E. M. v. Hornbostel, after R. Thurnwald, *Forschungen auf den Salomon-Inseln*, I, No. 22 and p. 487 f.

33a. Jaap Kunst, *Music in Flores*, 1942; the same, *Metre, Rhythm. Multi-Part Music*, 1950, p. 42.

33b. *Alleluja dilexit Andream*. After H. Husmann, *Die drei- und vierstimmigen Notre-Dame Organa*, 1940.

34a. A. Lavignac, *Encyclopédie de la musique*, I/2891.

34b. *New Oxford History of Music*, I, 1957, p. 172, Ex. 279.

35a. Kurt Reinhard, *Chinesische Musik*, 1956, p. 198.

35b. Same source as Ex. 6b, 205/1, p. 32, No. 48.

35c. D. I. Arakishvili, *Narodnaia pesna zapodonoi Gruzii (Imeretii)*, Moscow, 1908, after p. 124, No. 16.

36 and 37. W. A. Mozart, Symphony in G minor, K. 550, fourth movement.

38. R. Wagner, *Tristan und Isolde*, Introduction to Act III.

39. C. Debussy, *Images*, 1905–07.

40. A. Schoenberg, *Klavierstück*, Op. 33a.

41. R. Wagner, *Tristan und Isolde*, Introduction to Act I, m. 2 ff.; R. Wagner, *Das Rheingold*, m. 540; G. Mahler, Symphony No. 10, Adagio, rehearsal no. 28; A. Scriabin, "mystic chord"; B. Bartók, Piano Concerto No. 2, 2nd movement, m. 57; B. Bartók, Piano Concerto No. 2, 2nd movement, m. 94.

42a. Lorraine, recording, *Es wollt ein Jungknab auf Botschaft gehn*.

42b. Uckermark, Erk, *Deutsche Volkslieder*, 1838–45, III/1, No. 51, *Als ich gestern Abend auf der Gasse ging*.

43a. Recording, *Musique polynésienne*, Boîte à Musique LD 333.

43b. Jaap Kunst, article *Indonesische Musik*, MGG, VI, col. 1190.

43c. *Songs of New China*, Peking, 1953, p. 10 f.

44. I. Stravinsky, *Oedipus Rex*, revised ed., 1948, Hawkes Pocket Scores, p. 44.

45. I. Stravinsky, *The Rake's Progress*. Piano-vocal score by L. Spinnar, p. 196 f.

46a. L. van Beethoven, String Quartet in A minor, Op. 132.

46b. B. Bartók, Piano Concerto No. 3.

MUSICAL EXAMPLES

PRIMITIVE MELODY, STEPWISE AND TRIADIC

1 Indefinite steps, narrow range. Vedda of Ceylon

2 Fanfare melody. Pygmoids in highlands of New Guinea

3 Yodeling woman. Babinga Pygmies, Congo

COMMON ORIGIN IN LATE PALEOLITHIC HUNTING CIVILIZATIONS?

4 a. Bushmen   b. Lapps

5 a. Bushmen

b. Lapps   c. Lapps

STAMPING MELODIES AND ROUNDS, DESCENDING OCTAVE

6 a. Menominee Indians

b. Cheremisses (between the Volga and the Urals)   repeated several times

c. Italian *Laude*, 13th century   repeated twice with variants

ARCHAIC PASTORAL MELODY

7 a. Appenzell, 1545   b. Sweden

c. Caucasus   d. Japan

ARCHAIC EPIC MELODY

8   a. *Chanson de geste*   b. Russian *byline*

MELODIC FORMULAS OF ARCHAIC RITUAL SONGS

9   a. Jewish congregational song. Yemen   b. Gregorian Kyrie, Mass XVI

10   a. Babylonian synagogue chant   b. *Litania ad processionem*

11   a. Rigvedic song. India   b. Synagogue chant.

Yemen   c. Ambrosian *Pater noster*

12   a. Saman-Veda. India

b. and c. From Babylonian synagogue chants

13   a. Vedic song. India

b. Gregorian antiphon *(Sabbato ad Compl.)*

14   a. Muezzin's call. Algiers

b. Work song. Mallorca

JUBILUS, MELISMA, AND COLORATURA

15 a. Harvest song. Bulgaria

b. Work song. Gers (Southwestern France, near the Pyrenees)

c. Ambrosian Alleluia

16 Shepherd's song. Appenzell, 1798

17 Congregational melisma on "amen." Yemen

18 Coloratura. Persia

19 Coloratura. India

NOTATION AND IMPROVISATION

20 a. Chinese notation and a realization   b. Basse danse, c. 1470

21 From the Chaconne for unaccompanied violin. Max Reger

22 Precise transcription of a folk tune. Béla Bartók

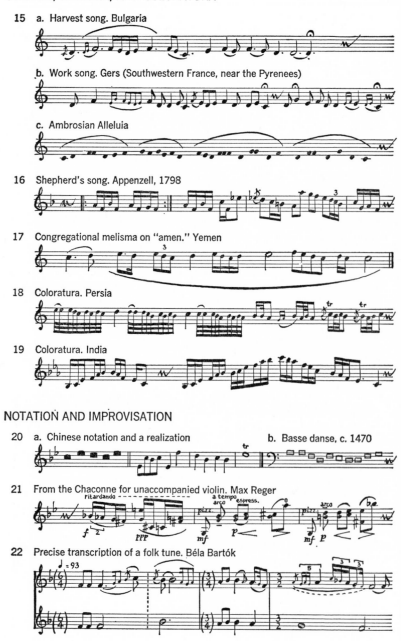

ANTIQUITY AND WIDE DISSEMINATION OF EIGHT-MEASURE TUNES

(three melodies in simple, regular meter, diatonic, descending octave)

23 a. Animal dance. North American Indians

b. Pamir, Central Asia

c. The Seikilos song (Epitaph, 1st century A.D.)

CHROMATICISM

24 a. Delphic hymn, 2nd century B.C.

b. *Gagaku,* Japanese court music

c. Gesualdo, Principe da Venosa, 1611 ("ò morire")

d. Beethoven, *Sonate Pathétique*   e. Wagner, *Tristan*

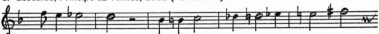

cresc.------------- *sfp*   *P*   *P*

DISTORTION AND RUPTURE OF THE LINE IN MODERN MUSIC

25   Anton Webern, String Quartet Op. 28, III.

IRREGULAR METERS

26   a. India. $3 + 2 + 2$

b. Turkey. $3 + 2 + 2 : + 3 + 4$

CHANGING METERS

27   a. Bulgarian folk tune

b. "Variable Meters." Boris Blacher, Piano Concerto Op. 42

SUBLIMATION OF THE RHYTHMIC PULSE

28   a. Dufay, *Christe eleison.* 15th century

b. Wagner, *Parsifal*

ABANDONMENT OF THE RHYTHMIC PULSE

29   a. Hindemith, *Cardillac.*

b. Ernst Krenek, Flute Piece.

NON-WESTERN POLYPHONY

30   a. Parallel fifths. Amazonas, Brazil   b. Parallel fourths. Amazonas, Brazil

31   Alternating fourths and fifths. Africa   32   Circling around a chord. South Seas

Canon over a Drone

33   a. Flores Island (Indonesia)

b. Notre Dame school (Paris), c. 1200

"Heterophony"

34   a. Algeria   b. Bali

Approach to "Polyphony"

35   a. China   b. Caucasus

c. Melismatic solo between two sustained tones. Caucasus

SUCCESSIONS OF CHORDS

Patterns from Early to Late Middle Ages

Logical Chord-Progression in the Modern West

Departure from Logical Chord-Progression

Dissonant Chords Since Wagner

LEVELING OUT OF EUROPEAN FOLK MELODY IN
MAJOR, SIMPLIFICATION OF METERS

42 Two versions of an old morning song

WORLDWIDE DISSEMINATION OF MELODY TYPES ORIGINALLY EUROPEAN

43 a. South Seas

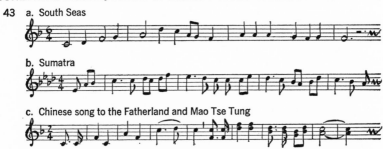

b. Sumatra

c. Chinese song to the Fatherland and Mao Tse Tung

OLD STYLES AS BASIS OF MODERN MUSIC

44 Stravinsky, "Clarissimus Oedipus, pollikeor divinabo"

45 Stravinsky, *The Rake's Progress*
The Devil (Nick) in banal diatonic writing with harpsichord

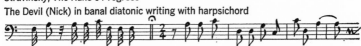

HISTORIC AND TRANSHISTORIC ASPECT

46 a. Beethoven, Quartet Op. 132. Thanksgiving song of a
convalescent to the Divinity, in the Lydian mode.   Molto adagio

sotto voce   cresc   *p*

b. Bartók, Third Piano Concerto. Adagio religioso

p   molto espr.; legato

A LIST OF RECENT PUBLICATIONS

ABBREVIATIONS:

AfMw = *Archiv für Musikwissenschaft*, Vol. IX–, 1952–.
Acta = *Acta Musicologica.* Quarterly Magazine of the International Musicological Society (formerly International Society of Musical Research), 1928–.
Mf = *Die Musikforschung*, 1948–.
MGG = *Die Musik in Geschichte und Gegenwart* (ed. by Friedrich Blume), Kassel, 1949–.

PRINCIPLES:

Wiora, Walter. *Herders Ideen zur Musikgeschichte*, in *Im Geiste Herders* (ed. by Erich Keyser), Kitzingen, 1953; *Schrift und Tradition als Quellen der Musikgeschichte*, in Congress Report Bamberg, 1953, Kassel, 1954; *Zur Grundlegung der Allgemeinen Musikgeschichte*, in *Deutsches Jahrbuch der Musikenwissenschaft*, I, 1956; *Musikwissenschaft und Universalgeschichte*, in *Acta*, XXXIII, 1961; *Idee und Methode "vergleichender" Musikforschung*, in Congress Report Salzburg, 1964, Kassel, 1964; and Hans Albrecht, *MGG* article, *Musikwissenschaft*.

SURVEYS AND ANTHOLOGIES:

Baines, Anthony, ed. *Musical Instruments*, Harmondsworth/Middlesex, 1961.
Besseler, Heinrich, and Max Schneider, eds. *Musikgeschichte in Bildern*, Leipzig, 1961–.
Buchner, Alexander. *Musikinstrumente im Wandel der Zeiten*, Prague, 1956.
Chailley, Jacques, ed. *Précis de musicologie*, Paris, 1958.
Collaer, Paul, and Albert van der Linden. *Atlas historique de la musique*, Paris, 1960.
Davison, A. T., and Willi Apel, eds. *Historical Anthology of Music*, 2 vols., Cambridge, Mass., 1946.
Engel, Hans. *Musik der Völker und Zeiten*, Darmstadt/Bonn/Bopard 1952; *Musik und Gesellschaft*, Berlin/Wunsiedel, 1960.
Fellerer, Gustav, ed. *Das Musikwerk. Eine Beispielsammlung zur Musikgeschichte*, Cologne, 1950–.
Handschin, Jacques. *Der Toncharakter*, Zurich, 1948; *Musikgeschichte im Überblick*, Lucerne, 2nd ed., 1964.
History of Music in Sound (Records by RCA).
Komma, M. K. *Musikgeschichte in Bildern*, Stuttgart, 1961.

Kutz, Adalbert. *Musikgeschichte und Tonsystematik*, Berlin, 1943 (*Neue deutsche Forschungen. Abteilung Musikwissenschaft*, XI).

New Oxford History of Music, London, 1954–.

Sachs, Curt. *Geist und Werden der Musikinstrumente*, Berlin, 1929; *The History of Musical Instruments*, New York, 1940; *The Commonwealth of Art*, New York, 1946; *Rhythm and Tempo*, New York, 1953; *A World History of the Dance*, London, 2nd ed., 1957.

Szabolcsi, Bence. *Bausteine zu einer Geschichte der Melodie*, Budapest, 1959.

I

PRE- AND EARLY HISTORY:

Broholm, H. C., W. P. Larsen, and Godtfred Skjerne. *The Lures of the Bronze Age*, Copenhagen, 1949.

Camp, C. M., and Bruno Nettl. *The Musical Bow in Southern Africa*, in *Anthropos. Internationale Zeitschrift fur Völker- und Sprachenkunde*, 50, 1955.

Danckert, Werner. *Wesen und Ursprung der Tonwelt im Mythos*, in *AfMw*, XII, 1955.

Emsheimer, Ernst. *Zur Ideologie der lappischen Zaubertrommel*, in *Ethnos*, IX, 1944; *Eine sibirische Parallele zur lappischen Zaubertrommel?* in *Ethnos*, XIII, 1948; *Studia ethnomusicologica eurasiatica*, Stockholm, 1964.

Fischer, Hans. *Schallgeräte in Ozeanien*, Strasbourg, 1958.

Häusler, Alexander. *Neue Funde steinzeitlicher Musikinstrumente in Osteuropa*, in *Acta*, XXXII, 1960.

MGG articles: *Flöteninstrumente, Horninstrumente*, etc.

Oldeberg, Andreas. *A Contribution to the History of the Scandinavian Bronze Lure in the Bronze and Iron Ages*, in *Acta archaeologica*, XVIII, 1947.

Schaeffner, André. *Origine des instruments de musique*, Paris, 1936.

Schneider, Marius. *Die musikalischen Beziehungen zwischen Urkulturen, Altpflanzern und Hirtenvölkern*, in *Zeitschrift für Ethnologie*, 70, 1938; *Die historischen Grundlagen der musikalischen Symbolik*, in *Mf*, IV, 1951; *Ist die vokale Mehrstimmigkeit eine Schöpfung der Altrassen?* in *Acta*, 23, 1951; *Les fondements intellectuels et psychologiques du chant magique*, in *Les Colloques de Wégimont*, I, 1954, Paris, 1956.

Seewald, Otto. *Beiträge zur Kenntnis der steinzeitlichen Musikinstrumente Europas*, Vienna, 1934; *Die Lyrendarstellungen der ostalpinen Hallstattkultur*, in *Festschrift Alfred Orel zum 70. Geburtstag*, Vienna/Wiesbaden, 1960.

Wiora, Walter. *Die vergleichende Frühgeschichte der europäischen*

Musik als methodische Forschung, in Congress Report Basel, 1949; *Zur Frühgeschichte der Musik in den Alpenländern*, Basel, 1949; *Musikgeschichte und Urgeschichte*, in *Festschrift für Carl-Allen Moberg, Svensk tidskrift för musikforskning*, 42, 1961.

Zerries, Otto. *Das Schwirrholz*, Stuttgart, 1942.

MUSIC OF PRIMITIVE PEOPLES AND ARCHAIC FOLK MUSIC:

Brailoiu, Constantin. *Collection universelle de musique populaire enregistrée* (Unesco); *Le Folklore musical*, in *Musica aeterna*, Zurich, 1949; *Le rhythme enfantin*, in *Les Colloques de Wégimont*, I, 1954, Paris, 1956.

Brandel, Rose. *The Music of Central Africa*, The Hague, 1961.

Les Colloques de Wégimont, I (1954), Paris, 1956 and III (1956), Paris, 1960.

Ethnomusicology. Journal of the Society for Ethnomusicology, 1957–.

Jones, A. M. *Studies in African Music*, 2 vols. London, 1959.

Journal of the International Folk Music Council, 1949–.

Kunst, Jaap. *Ethnomusicology*, The Hague, 3rd ed., 1959; Supplement, 1960.

MGG articles: *Albanien, Afrikanische Musik, Alpenmusik, Australien und Austronesien, Blasquinte, Buschmann- und Hottentotenmusik, Eskimo-Musik, Finnisch-ugrische Musik, Flores, Indianermusik, Jodeln, Lappen, Ostafrika, Ozeanien, Schlaginstrumente, Schwirrholz*, etc.

Nettl, Bruno. *Music in Primitive Culture*, Cambridge, 1956.

Sachs, Curt. *Vergleichende Musikwissenschaft. Musik der Fremdkulturen*, Heidelberg, 2nd ed., 1959.

Schneider, Marius. *Primitive Music*, in *New Oxford History of Music*, vol. I, London, 1957; *Ethnologische Musikforschung*, in *Lehrbuch der Völkerkunde* (Ed. by Leonhard Adam and Hermann Trimborn), Stuttgart, 3rd ed., 1957.

Wiora, Walter. *Europäischer Volksgesang. Gemeinsame Formen in charakteristischen Abwandlungen*, Cologne, 1952 (*Das Musikwerk*); *Älter als die Pentatonik*, in *Studia Memoriae Belae Bartok Sacra*, Budapest, 2nd ed., 1957; *Die Natur der Musik und die Musik der Naturvölker*, in *Journal of the International Folk Music Council*, 13, 1961.

II

ANTIQUITY:

Aign, Bernhard. *Die Geschichte der Musikinstrumente des ägäischen Raumes bis um 700 vor Christus*, Frankfurt/Main, 1963.

Becker, Oskar. *Frühgriechische Mathematik und Musiklehre,* in *AfMw,* XIV, 1957.

Behn, Friedrich. *Musikleben im Altertum und frühen Mittelalter,* Stuttgart, 1954.

Chailley, Jacques. *Le mythe des modes grecs,* in *Acta,* 28, 1956; *L'imbroglio des modes,* Paris, 1960.

Galpin, Francis. *The Music of the Sumerians,* Strasbourg, 2nd ed., 1955 (*Sammlung musikwissenschaftlicher Abhandlungen,* vol. 33).

Georgiades, Thrasybulos. *Der griechische Rhythmus,* Hamburg, 1949; *Musik und Rhythmus bei den Griechen,* Hamburg, 1958.

Gombosi, Otto. *Tonarten und Stimmungen der antiken Musik,* Copenhagen, 1939 (reprint 1951).

Hartmann, Henrike. *Die Musik der sumerischen Kultur,* Frankfurt/Main, 1960 (dissertation).

Hickmann, Hans. *Musicologie pharaonique,* Strasbourg, 1956; *Les problèmes et l'état actuel des recherches musicologiques en Egypte,* in *Acta,* 28, 1956; *Musikerziehung im alten Ägypten,* in *Musikererkenntnis und Musikerziehung. Dankesgabe für Hans Mersmann,* Kassel, 1957; *La chironomie dans l'Egypte pharaonique,* in *Zeitschrift für ägyptische Sprache und Altertumskunde* 83/2, 1958.

Huchzermayer, Helmut. *Aulos und Kithara in der griechischen Musik bis zum Ausgang der klassischen Zeit,* Emsdetten, 1931 (dissertation).

Hunger, Herbert. *Lexikon der griechischen und römischen Mythologie,* Vienna, 1953.

Husmann, Heinrich. *Antike und Orient in ihrer Bedeutung für die europäische Musik,* Congress Report Hamburg, 1956, Kassel, 1957; *Grundlagen der antiken und orientalischen Musikkultur,* Berlin, 1961.

Koller, Hermann. *Musik und Dichtung im alten Griechenland,* Berne/Munich, 1963.

Martin, Emile. *Essai sur les rhythmes de la chanson grecques antique,* Paris, 1953.

MGG articles: *Ägyptische Musik, Ethos, Etrurien, Griechenland, Handzeichen, Hethitische Musik,* etc.

Otto, W. F. *Die Musen und der göttliche Ursprung des Singens und Sagens,* Düsseldorf, 1955.

Pöhlmann, Egert. *Griechische Musikfragmente,* Nuremberg, 1960.

Richter, Lukas. *Die Aufgaben der Musiklehre nach Aristoxenos und Klaudios Ptolemaios,* in *AfMw,* 15, 1958; *Zur Wissenschaftslehre von der Musik bei Platon und Aristoteles,* Berlin, 1961.

Sachs, Curt. *The Rise of Music in the Ancient World,* New York, 1943.

Schlesinger, Kathleen. *The Greek Aulos,* London, 1939.

Stauder, Wilhelm. *Die Harfen und Leiern der Sumerer*, Frankfurt/ Main, 1957.

Van der Waerden, L. *Harmonielehre der Pythagoräer*, in *Hermes, Zeitschrift für classische Philologie*, 78, 1943.

Vetter, Walther. *Aufsätze zur antiken Musik*, in *Mythos-Melos-Musica*, I, Leipzig, 1957.

Vogel, Martin. *Die Enharmonik der Griechen*, 2 vols. Düsseldorf, 1963 (*Orpheus*, III–IV).

Wegener, Max. *Das Musikleben der Griechen*, Berlin, 1949; *Die Musikinstrumente des alten Orients*, Münster, 1950.

Wille, Günther. *Die Bedeutung der Musik im Leben der Römer*, Tübingen, 1953 (typescript); *Zur Musikalität der alten Römer*, in *AfMw*, 11, 1954.

Winnington-Ingram, R. P. *Ancient Greek Music 1932–1957* (Lustrum III, 1958).

JEWISH, EARLY CHRISTIAN, AND EASTERN CHRISTIAN MUSIC:

Gerson-Kiwi, Edith. *Musique dans la Bible*, in *Dictionnaire de la Bible* ed. by Pirot, Suppl. Bd. V, Paris, 1957; *Musik der Bibel in der Tradition althebräischer Melodien* (Schwann Recording AMS 5004).

Handschin, Jacques. *Das Zeremonienwerk Kaiser Konstantins und die sangbare Dichtung*, Basel, 1942; *Le chant ecclésiastique russe*, in *Acta*, 24, 1952; *Gesungene Apologetik*, and other papers, in *Gedenkschrift Jacques Handschin*, Berne/Stuttgart, 1957.

MGG articles: *Armenische, Äthiopische, Byzantinische, Frühchristliche, Jüdische Musik*, etc.

Söhngen, Oskar. *Theologische Grundlagen der Kirchenmusik*, in *Leiturgia. Handbuch des evangelischen Gottesdienstes*, vol. IV, Kassel, 1961.

Tillyard, H. J. W. *Gegenwärtiger Stand der byzantinischen Musikforschung*, in *Mf*, VII, 1954.

Wellesz, Egon. *A History of Byzantine Music and Hymnography*, Oxford, 1949, 2nd ed., 1960.

Werner, Eric. *New Studies in the History of the Early Octoechos*, Congress Report Utrecht, 1952, Amsterdam, 1953; *Musical Aspects of the Dead Sea Scrolls*, in *The Musical Quarterly*, 43/1, 1957; *The Sacred Bridge*, London/New York, 1958.

Wessely, Othmar. *Die Musikanschauung des Abtes Pambo*, in *Anzeiger der phil.-hist. Klasse der österreichen Akademie der Wissenschaften, Jahrgang* 1952 Nr. 4, vol. 89, Vienna, 1952.

ORIENTAL MUSIC:

Bake, Arnold. *Die beiden Tongeschlechter bei Bharata*, Congress Report Lüneburg, 1950, Kassel.

Bibliography of Asiatic Musics, compiled by Richard A. Waterman and others, in *Notes,* V–VIII, 1947–51.

Chung Sik Keh. *Die koreanische Musik,* Strasbourg, 1935.

Daniélou, Alain. *Northern Indian Music,* 2 vols. London/Calcutta, 1949; *Traité de musicologie comparée,* Paris, 1959; (ed.) *A Musical Anthology of the Orient* (Unesco Collection, Record BM 30 L 2001–06).

Eckhardt, Hans. *Das Kokonchomonshû des Tachibana Narisue als musikgeschichtliche Quelle,* Wiesbaden, 1956, in *Göttinger Asiatische Forschungen,* VI.

Emsheimer, Ernst. *Music of Eastern Mongolia,* in *Reports from the Scientific Expedition to the North-Western Provinces of China under the Leadership of Dr. Sven Hedin,* Publication 21, Stockholm, 1943.

d'Erlanger, Baron Rodolphe. *La musique arabe,* 6 vols. Paris, 1930–59.

Farmer, H. G. *Oriental Studies*—mainly musical, London/New York, 1953.

Harich-Schneider, Eta. *The Earliest Sources of Chinese Music and Their Survival in Japan,* Tokyo, 1955 (*Monumenta Nipponica,* XI).

Hood, Mantle. *The Nuclear Theme as a Determinant of Patet in Javanese Music,* Groningen, 1954.

Journal of the Society for Research in Asiatic Music, 1938–41, and 1951–.

Kunst, Jaap. *Music in Java,* The Hague, 1949; *The Cultural Background of Indonesian Music* (Mededeling 82 van het Koninklijk "Indisch Instituut," Amsterdam), 1949; *Cultural Relations between the Balkans and Indonesia,* Amsterdam, 2nd ed., 1960 (Mededelingen van het Koninklijk Instituut voor de Tropen, vol. 107).

Malm, William. *Japanese Music and Musical Instruments,* Tokyo, 1959; *Nagauta. The Heart of Kabuki Music,* Rutland/Tokyo, 1963.

May, Elizabeth. *The Influence of the Meiji Period on Japanese Children's Music,* Berkeley/Los Angeles, 1963 (University of California Publications in Music, vol. VI).

Marcel-Dubois, Claudie. *Les instruments de musique de l'Inde ancienne,* Paris, 1941.

MGG articles: *Afghanistan, Arabien, Asiatische Musik, Bali, Chinesische Musik, Gamelang, Gong, Hindu-Javanische, Indische, Indonesische, Japanische, Javanische Musik, Mongolen, Nordafrikanische, Persische Musik, Raga-Maqam-Nomos,* etc.

Reinhard, Kurt. *Die Musik Birmas,* Würzburg, 1939 (*Schriftenreihe des musikwissenschaftlichen Seminars der Universität München,* V); *Chinesische Musik,* Kassel/Eisenach, 1956; *Turkische Musik,* Kassel/Eisenach, 1962.

Sambamoorthy, P.   *South Indian Music*, 5 vols., Madras University, 1950.
Swāmī Prajnanananda.   *Historical Development of Indian Music*, Calcutta, 1960.
Trân Van Khê.   *La musique vietnamienne traditionelle*, Paris, 1962.
Trefgzer, Heins.   *Das Musikleben der Tang-Zeit*, in *Sinica*, XIII, Frankfurt/Main, 1938.

III

GENERAL:

Grout, D. J.   *A History of Western Music*, New York, 1960.
Lang, P. H.   *Music in Western Civilization*, New York, 1941.
Mersmann, Hans.   *Musikgeschichte in der abendländischen Kultur*, Frankfurt/Main, 1955.
Preussner, Eberhard.   *Musikgeschichte des Abendlandes*, Vienna, 2nd ed., 1958.
Wiora, Walter.   *Europäische Volkmusik und abendländische Tonkunst*, Kassel, 1957; *Die geschichtliche Sonderstellung der abendländischen Musik*, in *Musik und Musikerziehung in der Reifezeit. Vorträge der 3. Bundesschulmusikwoche*, ed. by Egon Kraus, Mainz, 1959.

BEGINNINGS:

Husmann, Heinrich.   *Sequenz und Prosa*, in *Annales musicologiques*, II, 1954; *Das System der modalen Rhythmik*, in *AfMw*, XI, 1954; *Alleluia, Vers und Sequenz*, in *Annales musicologiques*, IV, 1956.
Jammers, Ewald.   *Der mittelalterliche Choral*, Mainz, 1954; *Anfänge der abendländischen Musik*, Strasbourg, 1955; *Musik in Byzanz, im päpstlichen Rom und im Frankenreich*, Heidelberg, 1962.
MGG articles: *Alleluja, Antiphon, Choral, Gloria, Graduale, Gregorianik, Hymnus, Psalm*, etc.
Schneider, Marius.   *A proposito del influjo arabe*, in *Anuario Musical*, I, Barcelona, 1946; *Arabischer Einfluss in Spanien?*, in Congress Report, Bamberg, 1953, Kassel, 1954; *Wurzeln und Anfänge der abendländischen Mehrstimmigkeit*, in Congress Report New York, 1961, Kassel, 1961.
Waite, William.   *The Rhythm of Twelfth-Century Polyphony*, New Haven, 1954; *The Era of Melismatic Polyphony*, in Congress Report New York, 1961, Kassel, 1961.
Wellesz, Egon.   *Eastern Elements in Western Chant*, Boston, 1947 (*Monumenta musicae byzantinae*. American Series I).

INTERSECTIONS AND DEVELOPMENTAL TRAITS:

Apel, Willi. *The Notation of Polyphonic Music,* Cambridge, Mass. 5th ed., 1953.

Bandmann, Günther. *Melancholie und Musik. Ikonographische Studien,* Cologne/Opladen, 1960.

Barbour, J. Murray. *Tuning and Temperament,* Michigan, 1953.

Besseler, Heinrich. *Singstil und Instrumentalstil in der europäischen Musik,* in Congress Report Bamberg, 1953, Kassel, 1954; *Das musikalische Hören der Neuzeit,* Berlin, 1959.

Eggebrecht, H. H. *Studien zur musikalischen Terminologie,* Wiesbaden, 1955.

Einstein, Alfred. *Greatness in Music,* New York, 1941.

Georgiades, Thrasybulos. *Musik und Sprache. Das Werden der abendländischen Musik, dargestellt an der Vertonung der Messe,* Berlin/Göttingen/Heidelberg, 1954.

Gurlitt, Wilibald. *Musik und Rhetorik (Helicon,* V 1944); *Form in der Musik als Zeitgestaltung,* Wiesbaden, 1954.

Hermann-Bengen, Irmgard. *Tempobezeichnungen. Ursprung-Wandel im 17. und 18. Jahrhundert,* Tutzing, 1959.

Machabey, Armand. *Genèse de la tonalité musicale classique des origines au XVe siècle,* Paris, 1955.

MGG articles: *Notation, Diatonik-Chromatik-Enharmonik, Konsonanz-Dissonanz, Dreiklang, Dur-Moll, Kadenz und Klausel, Kontrapunkt, Cantus firmus, Kanon, Harmonielehre, Dynamik, Instrumentation,* etc.; *Form, Komposition, Chorkomposition,* etc.; *Musikästhetik, Figuren, Musica theorica-practica-poetica,* etc.

Müller-Blattau, Joseph. *Gestaltung-Umgestaltung. Studien zur Geschichte der musikalischen Variation,* Stuttgart, 1950; *Das Verhältnis von Wort und Ton in der Geschichte der Musik,* Stuttgart, 1952.

Pohlmann, Hansjörg. *Die Frühgeschichte des musikalischen Urheberrechts,* Kassel, 1962.

Riedel, Herbert. *Musik und Musikerlebnis in der erzählenden deutschen Dichtung,* Bonn, 1959.

Schoolfield, G. C. *The Figure of the Musician in German Literature,* Chapel Hill, 1956 (University of North Carolina Studies in the Germanic Languages and Literatures, 19).

Smits van Waesberghe. *A Textbook of Melody. A Course in Functional Melodic Analysis,* Rome, 1955.

Unger, Hans-Heinrich. *Die Beziehungen zwischen Musik und Rhetorik im 16.–18. Jahrhundert.* Würzburg, 1941.

Wiora, Walter. *Musica poetica und musikalisches Kunstwerk,* in *Festschrift Karl Gustav Fellerer zum 60. Geburtstag,* Regensburg, 1962.

EPOCHS, TRENDS, GENRES:

L'Ars nova, Paris, 1959 (*Les Colloques de Wégimont*, II, 1955).
Benary, Peter. *Die deutsche Kompositionslehre des 18. Jahrhunderts.* Leipzig [1960].
Besseler, Heinrich. *Bourdon und Fauxbourdon. Studien zum Ursprung der niederländischen Musik.* Leipzig, 1950.
Brook, Barry S. *La Symphonie française dans la seconde moitié du XVIIIᵉ siècle*, 3 vols. Paris, 1962.
Brown, Howard M. *Music in the French Secular Theater* (*1400–1550*), Cambridge, Mass., 1963.
Bukofzer, Manfred. *Music in the Baroque Era*, New York, 1947.
Chailley, Jacques. *Histoire musicale du Moyen Age*, Paris, 1950.
Chanson and Madrigal, Studies in Comparison and Contrasts (ed. by J. Haar), Cambridge, Mass., 1964.
Clercx, Susanne. *Le Baroque et la musique. Essai d'esthétique musicale*, Brussels, 1948. *Johannes Ciconia. Un musicien liégeois et son temps*, 2 vols. Brussels, 1960.
Dolmetsch, Arnold. *The Interpretation of the Music of the XVII and XVIII Centuries*, London [1946].
Donington, Robert. *The Interpretation of Early Music*, London, 1963.
Eggebrecht, Hans Heinrich. *Barock als musikgeschichtliche Epoche*, in *Aus der Welt des Barock*, Stuttgart, 1957.
Einstein, Alfred. *Music in the Romantic Era*, New York, 1947; *The Italian Madrigal*, 3 vols., Princeton, 1949.
Fischer, Kurt von. *Studien zur italienischen Musik des Trecento und frühen Quattrocento*, Berne, 1956.
Grout, Donald J. *A Short History of Opera*, 2 vols., New York, 1947.
Guichard, Léon. *La musique et les lettres au temps du romantisme*, Paris, 1955.
Hammerstein, Reinhold. *Die Musik der Engel. Untersuchungen zur Musikanschauung des Mittelalters*, Berne/Munich, 1962.
Kerman, Joseph. *The Elizabethan Madrigal. A Comparative Study*, New York, 1962.
Martinez, Marie Louise. *Die Musik des frühen Trecento*, Tutzing, 1963.
Meyer, Ernst Hermann. *English Chamber Music*, London, 2nd ed., 1951.
MGG articles: *Notre-Dame-Epoche, Ars antiqua, Ars nova, Modus, Discantus, Conductus, Estampie, Minnesang, Liturgische Dramen, Historie, Fauxbourdon*, etc.; *Humanismus, Messe, Motette, Madrigal, Gemeindegesang, Choralbearbeitung, Calvinistische Musik, Jesuiten*, etc.; *Renaissance, Barock, Absolutismus, Aufklärung, Freimaurer-*

musik, Klassik, Romantik; Oper, Bühnenmusik, Oratorium, Passion, Kantate, Lied, Chanson, Ballade, Klaviermusik, Fuge, Fantasie, Concerto grosso, Konzert, Kammermusik, Nationalhymnen, Männerchor, etc.

Müller-Blattau, Joseph. *Geschichte der Fuge,* Kassel, 3rd ed., 1963.

Newman, William S. *The Sonata in the Baroque Era,* Chapel Hill, 1959.

Noske, Frits. *La mélodie française de Berlioz à Duparc,* Paris, 1954.

Reese, Gustave. *Music in the Middle Ages,* New York, 1940; *Music in the Renaissance,* New York, 1954.

Salmen, Walter. *Die Schichtung der mittelalterlichen Musikkultur in der ostdeutschen Grenzlage,* Kassel, 1954; *Der fahrende Musiker im europäischen Mittelalter,* Kassel, 1960.

Schrade, Leo. *Renaissance: The Historical Conception of Epoch,* in Congress Report Utrecht, 1952, Amsterdam, 1953.

Stäblein-Harder, Hanna. *Fourteenth-Century Mass Music in France,* Rome, 1962.

Stevenson, Robert. *Spanish Cathedral Music in the Golden Age,* Berkeley/Los Angeles, 1961.

PEOPLES AND COUNTRIES:

Handschin, Jacques. Articles about Russian Music, in *Gedenkschrift Jacques Handschin,* Berne/Stuttgart, 1957.

Komma, Karl Michael. *Das böhmische Musikantentum,* Kassel, 1960.

MGG articles: *Basken, Belgien, Bulgarische Musik, Dänemark, Deutschland, England, Finnland, Frankreich, Irische Musik, Island, Italien, Jugoslawien, Niederländische Musik, Norwegen, Österreich, Polen, Portugal, Russland, Schweden, Schweiz,* etc.

Mooser, Robert-Aloys. *Annales de la musique et des musiciens en Russie au XVIII⁸ siècle,* 3 vols., Geneva, 1948–51.

Moser, Hans Joachim. *Die Tonsprachen des Abendlandes,* Berlin, 1960.

Musik des Ostens. Sammelbände für historische und vergleichende Forschung, Kassel, 1962–.

Musique russe (ed. by Pierre Souvtchinsky), 2 vols., Paris, 1953.

Wiora, Walter. *Über die sogenannten nationalen Schulen der osteuropäischen Musik,* in *Syntagma Friburgense. Historische Studien Hermann Aubin dargebracht zum 70. Geburtstag,* Lindau/Constance, 1956.

IV

SERIALS (A) BOOKS:

Darmstädter Beiträge zur Neuen Musik (ed. by Wolfgang Steincke

and Ernst Thomas), Mainz, 1958–.
Die Reihe. Information über serielle Musik (ed. by Herbert Eimert and others), Vienna/Zurich/London, 1955–.
Kommentare zur Neuen Musik, I (articles from *Die Reihe* I–VII), Cologne, 1960.
Kontrapunkte. Schriften zur deutschen Musik der Gegenwart (ed. by Heinrich Lindlar) Rodenkirchen/Rhein, 1958–.
Musik der Zeit (ed. by Heinrich Lindlar and Reinhold Schubert), Bonn, 1952–.
Musikalische Zeitfragen (ed. by Walter Wiora), Kassel, 1956–.

(B) JOURNALS:
Melos; Musica; The World of Music; Hausmusik, vols. I–XXII, 1932–58.
Junge Musik, vols. I–VIII, 1950–57; *Kontakte*, vols. IX–, 1958–.
Modern Music, vols. I–XXIII, 1924–46; *Perspectives of New Music*, vols. I–, 1963–.

GENERAL BOOKS:
Adorno, Theodor W. *Dissonanzen. Musik in der verwalteten Welt*, Göttingen, 1956; *Philosophie der neuen Musik*, Frankfurt, 2nd ed., 1958; *Klangfiguren*, Frankfurt, 1959.
Collaer, Paul. *La musique moderne*, Brussels, 2nd ed., 1958.
Doflein, Erich. *Vielfalt und Zwiespalt in unserer Musik* (*Musikalische Zeitfragen*, IX, 1960).
Erpf, Hermann. *Vom Wesen der Neuen Musik*, Stuttgart, 1949; *Gegenswartskunde der Musik*, Mainz, 1954; *Tagesfragen des Musiklebens*, Stuttgart, 1957; *Wie soll es weitergehen?* Rodenkirchen/Rhein, 1958 (*Kontrapunkte*, III); *Vielfalt und Zwiespalt in unserer Musik* (*Musikalische Zeitfragen*, IX, 1960).
Honolka, Kurt. *Das vielstimmige Jahrhundert. Musik in unserer Zeit*, Stuttgart, 1960.
Kirchmeyer, Helmut. *Igor Strawinsky. Zeitgeschichte im Persönlichkeitsbild*. Regensburg, 1958.
Mersmann, Hans. *Neue Musik des XX. Jahrhunderts im Spiegel des Weltgeschehens*, Rodenkirchen/Rhein, 1958 (*Kontrapunkte*, I).
Prisma der gegenwärtigen Musik. (ed. by Joachim E. Berendt and Jürgen Uhde), Hamburg, 1959.
Stuckenschmidt, Hans Heinz. *Neue Musik*, Frankfurt/Main, 1951 (*Zwischen den beiden Weltkriegen*, II).
Wörner, Karl Heinrich. *Neue Musik in der Entscheidung*, Mainz, 2nd ed., 1956.

SECTIONS:

Berton, Walter Michael. *Musik und Mikrophon*, Düsseldorf, 1951.

Brelet, Gisèle. *Le temps musical*, Paris, 1949; *L'Interprétation créatrice*, Paris, 1951.

Ehmann, Wilhelm. *Erbe und Auftrag musikalischer Erneuerung*, Kassel, 1956.

Internationales Handbuch für Rundfunk und Fernsehen, Hamburg, 1957–.

Kraus, Egon, ed. *Berichte über die Bundesschulmusikwochen:* I, *Musikerziehung in der Schule*, Mainz, 1955; II, *Musik als Lebenshilfe*, Hamburg, 1958; III, *Musik und Musikerziehung in der Reifezeit*, Mainz [1959]; IV, *Musik und Bildung in unserer Zeit*, Mainz, 1961; *The Present State of Music Education in the World* (International Society for Music Education), 1961.

MGG articles: *Atonalität, Elektrische Musikinstrumente, Elektronische Musik, Expressionismus, Filmmusik, Gesellschaften und Vereine, Impressionismus, Jugendmusik, Konzertwessen, Mechanische Musikinstrumente, Musikerziehung, Musikkritik, Musikverlag und Musikalienhandel, Organization, Rundfunk und Fernsehen,* etc.

Moles, Abraham A. *Les musiques expérimentales*, Paris/Zurich/Brussels, 1960.

Musik in der Medizin. Beiträge zur Musiktherapie (ed. by Hildebrand Richard Teirich), Stuttgart, 1958.

Musikpädagogische Bibliothek (founded by Leo Kestenberg, continued by Eberhard Preussner), Heidelberg, 1959–.

Olkhovsky, Andrey. *Music under the Soviets; the Agony of an Art*, New York, 1955.

Pfrogner, Hermann. *Die Zwölfordnung der Töne*. Zurich/Leipzig/Vienna, 1953; *Der zerrissene Orpheus*, Frieburg/Munich, 1957.

Prieberg, Fred K. *Musik des technischen Zeitalters*, Zurich/Frieberg, 1956.

Schmidt-Joos, Siegfried. *Geschäfte mit Schlagern*, Bremen, 1960.

Silbermann, Alphons. *La musique, la radio et l'auditeur*, Paris, 1954; *Wovon lebt die Musik? Die Prinzipien der Musiksoziologie*, Regensburg, 1957.

Schulze, Erich. *Urheberrecht in der Musik und die deutsche Urheberrechtsgesellschaft*, Berlin, 2nd ed., 1956.

Stephen, Rudolf. *Neue Musik. Versuch einer kritischen Einführung*. Göttingen, 1958.

Vincent, John. *The Diatonic Modes in Modern Music*, Los Angeles, 3rd ed., 1957.

Winckel, Fritz, ed. *Klangstruktur der Musik*, Berlin, 1955; *Die Grenzen der musikalischen Perzeption unter besonderer Berücksichtigung der elektronischen Musik*, in *AfMw*, XV, 1958: *Phänomene des musikalischen Hörens*, Berlin/Wunsiedel, 1960.

Wiora, Walter. *Musik im Wandel von Freizeit und Bildung*, 2nd ed., 1958; *Der Untergang des Volksliedes und sein zweites Dasein*, in *Das Volkslied heute* (*Musikalische Zeitfragen*, VII, 1959).

EXTRA-EUROPEAN DEVELOPMENT:

Chase, Gilbert. *America's Music. From the Pilgrims to the Present*, New York/Toronto/London, 1955.

Correa de Azevedo, Luiz Heitor, and Charles Seeger. *The Cultivation of Various European Traditions in the Americas*, in Congress Report New York, 1961, Kassel, 1961.

Dauer, Alfons M. *Der Jazz*, Kassel, 1958.

Eckardt, Hans. *Die Ausbreitung abendländischer Musik in Japan*, 1962.

Harich-Schneider, Eta. *The Present Condition of Japanese Court Music*, in *The Musical Quarterly*, 39, 1935.

Hodeir, André. *Jazz: Its Evolution and Essence*, New York/London, 1956.

Lang, Paul Henry, ed. *One Hundred Years of Music in America*, New York, 1961.

Mersmann, Hans. *Notizen von einer Japanreise*, in *Musica*, XI/2, 1957.

MGG articles: *Amerika, Kanada, Lateinamerika, Volksmusik, Mittelamerika, Negermusik in den Vereinigten Staaten*, etc. See also articles listed under Oriental Music, II above.

Mueller, John L. *The American Symphony Orchestra: A Social History of Musical Taste*, Bloomington, 1951.

Schneerson, Georg. *Die Musikkultur Chinas*, Leipzig, 1955.

Slonimsky, Nicolas. *Music of Latin America*, New York, 2nd ed., 1950.

Subirá, José and Antoine E. Cherbulies. *Musikgeschichte von Spanien, Portugal, Lateinamerika*, Zurich/Stuttgart [1957].

Waterman, Richard. *Tribal, Folk and Café Music of West Africa*, Field Recordings New York, 1950; *African Influence in the Music of the Americas*, in *Proceedings of the XXIXth International Congress of Americanists*, 1951.

INDEX

Abaton, 54
accompagnamento obbligato, 132
Achilles, 76
Adorno, T. W., 151, 166, 173, 181n, 189
Aeschylus, 71
Ages, primitive:
  Stone Age, 17–19, 22, 24–26, 28, 36, 40
  Neolithic (Ceramic) Age, 18, 29–36
  Megalithic Age, 18, 25, 33
  Bronze Age, 18, 36
  Iron Age, 18, 36
  Upper Stone Age, 20–21, 23
  Lower Stone Age, 24
  Late Paleolithic Age, 27
  Paleolithic Age, 29–31
  Protolithic Age, 27
  Mesolithic Age, 31
Agon (Stravinsky), 166
Aïda (Verdi), 53
Akh-en-Aton, 54
Alcaeus, 83
Alcman, 83
Al-Farabi, 120
Alkaios, 71
Alleluia, 93–94
Amen, 94
Amenophis, 34
American music, 153–54
  role of the American Negro in, 158
  jazz and, 158–61, 167
Ammon, 55
Antigone (Orff), 171
Apollo, 25, 73–74
Apollon Musagète (Stravinsky), 171
Arabic maqam. See maqam; Orient, music in
Arabic music theory, 104
  quarter tone system, 106
Arabo-Islamic culture, music in
  origins, 117–18
  predilection for solo and chamber music, 119–20

ornamentation in, 120
vocal and chamber music in, 120
scales in, 120
use of microtones in, 120–21
polyphony in, 121
forms of, 121
instruments, 121
Archives of Musical Recordings, Jerusalem, 91
Aristoxenos, 78–79, 81
Assurbanipal, 53
Assyria, 49, 53–54, 62, 68
astrology, influence on music of early high cultures, 67–68
Aton, 54
atonality, 175, 177. See also serial music
aulos, 64, 74, 76, 81, 83
Aurignacian period, 27, 34

Bach, J. S., 127–29, 138–39, 142–43, 152, 169–70, 177
  Passions, 134
Bacon, Francis, 139
Bake, Arnold, 103
Bartók, Béla, 141, 165, 169–70, 177
Beethoven, Ludwig van, 135, 144, 149, 157, 162, 168
Behn, Friedrich, 17, 33, 51
Berlioz, Hector, 143–44
Bernauerin, Die (Orff), 181
Bharata, 102, 106
Bible, The, 91
biwa (Japanese lute), 116
Bizet, Georges, 140
Blacher, Boris, 179
Boethius, 75, 86, 127
Bortniansky, Dmitri, 140
"Brahma," 101, 107–08
Brahms, Johannes, 135, 140, 142
Brecht, Bert, 172
Breuil, Henri, 22
Britten, Benjamin, 164
Bronze Age, 18, 36
Brubeck, Dave, 161